BEYOND THEOLOGY

Also by Alan Watts

ALAN WATTS

BEYOND THEOLOGY

The Art of Godmanship

VINTAGE BOOKS

A Division of Random House
New York

The author wishes to thank the following authors and publishers for permission to include copyright material: James Nisbet and Company, Ltd. and Harper & Row, Publishers, for excerpt from *Worship* by Evelyn Underhill. Faber & Faber, Ltd. and Harcourt, Brace & World, Inc., for excerpt from "Five-Finger Exercises" from *Collected Poems 1909–1962* by T. S. Eliot and for excerpt from "East Coker, III" from *Four Quartets* by T. S. Eliot. Sheed & Ward Inc. for excerpts from *The Spiritual Letters of Dom John Chapman* by Dom John Chapman. Published by Sheed & Ward Inc., 1946. John Murray (Publishers) Ltd., London, and Houghton Mifflin Company, Boston, for excerpts from "An 18th Century Calvinist Hymn" and "Before the Anaesthetic" now appearing in John Betjeman's *Collected Poems*. S. P. C. K., London, and The Macmillan Company, New York, for excerpt from *Hebrew Religion* by W. O. E. Oesterley and Theodore H. Robinson. Miss D. E. Collins and J. M. Dent & Sons Ltd. for "The Mirror of Madmen" from *The Wild Knight and Other Poems* by G. K. Chesterton. This selection also appears in *The Collected Poems of G. K. Chesterton* published by Dodd, Mead & Company. Cover illustration reprinted from *Psychology Today* Magazine, January 1973, © Communications/Research/Machines, Inc.

Library of Congress Cataloging in Publication Data

Watts, Alan Wilson, 1915–
Beyond theology.

Bibliography: p.
1. Christianity and other religions. I. Title
[BR127.W28 1973]   261.2   73–4542

ISBN 0–394–71923–9

Manufactured in the United States of America

TO MY FATHER,
Laurence Wilson Watts

CONTENTS

PREFACE

Perhaps I can best indicate the spirit and approach of
this book by asking you to imagine that you are attending a solemn service in a great cathedral, complete with candles, incense, chanting monks, and
priests in vestments of white, scarlet and shimmering
gold. Suddenly someone pulls you by the sleeve and
says, "Psst! Come out back. I've got something to
show you." You follow him out by the west door, and
then go around the building to the extreme east end
where there is a small door leading into the sacristy
or vestry. This is the ecclesiastical equivalent of the
green room in the theater, and you are about to enter
by what, in a worldly setting, would be called the
stage door. However, just outside you notice a couple
of clerics—in their vestments—lighting up cigarettes. Now transpose this scene to Heaven, so that
the church service will be nothing less than the worship of the saints and angels around the throne of

the Lord God of Hosts. I pull your sleeve and say, "Psst!"

I am afraid that there are those who will feel not only that this is not very reverent, but also that such an approach is absolutely blasphemous, and that no one could possibly be saying, "Psst!" in front of the throne of God except, perhaps, the Devil himself. However, the reader must be assured that it is far from my intention to debunk, to give offense, or to hold sacred things up to ridicule. For your author is acting, not in the role of the Devil, but in the capacity of the Court Jester, and I am sure that there must be such an office even (or especially) in Heaven.

If you know anything about the lore and the history of the Fool at Court, you will know that his function was not merely to be funny. I am not about to build you a convenient slide into religion, greased with wit. The function of the Fool was to keep his monarch human and, with luck, even humane, by a judicious unstuffing of his pomposity and by keeping alive his sense of humor—the essence of which is laughter *at oneself*. Undoubtedly the Lord God is not in need of these services. Nevertheless, omnipotent and self-sufficient as he is held to be, he is alleged to have an immense entourage of ministering angels, doing things which he could very well take care of himself, and without the least exertion. Theologians call this unbusiness-like arrangement the "divine economy," because the economics of Heaven are based, not on saving and scraping, but on the utmost extravagance and exuberance—as witness the proverbial prodigality of nature. In Heaven (and also, if we could see it aright, on Earth) everything is gloriously unnecessary, and this would include the office and work of the totally unnecessary Fool.

This book might, then, have been entitled *Inside Theology* or even *Inside Heaven,* were it not that these *Inside* titles have been pre-empted by Mr. John Gunther. Because it does not presume to be a scholarly book, I am not using such technical hellenisms as *Metatheology* or *Paratheology*,[1] though *Beyond Theology* is an approximate translation of the former used in somewhat the same sense as "metalanguage" —that is, a language$_2$ designed to discuss a language$_1$ from a higher level of abstraction or from a larger frame of reference. It is intended that in "The Art of Godmanship" there shall be the echo, not only of Stephen Potter, but also of the "Godmanhood" of Solovyev and Berdyaev.

I have previously published three other theological books: *Behold the Spirit* (1947), *The Supreme Identity* (1950), and *Myth and Ritual in Christianity* (1953). In varying ways these books attempted a synthesis between traditional Christianity and the unitive mysticism of Hinduism and Buddhism, and in this respect *The Supreme Identity* was probably the most successful. It represented a point of view which is associated with the work of Ananda Coomaraswamy, René Guénon, Frithjof Schuon, Marco Pallis, and Alain Daniélou—the so-called "traditionalist school" which regards every orthodox spiritual tradition as a more-or-less deliberate adaptation of the *philosophia perennis* to the needs of different cul-

[1] My next-door neighbor, the Greek painter Varda, has suggested also catatheology, anatheology, prostheology, epitheology, apotheology, peritheology, hypertheology, hypotheology, and atheology.

tures. They incline to see the purest form of this perennial wisdom in the non-dualist (*advaita*) Vedanta,
which is the central viewpoint (*darshan*) of Hinduism.

Upon reflection, this did not satisfy me. There is
not a scrap of evidence that the Christian hierarchy
was ever aware of itself as one among several lines
of transmission for a universal tradition. Christians,
whether of the right wing of the Catholics or the left
wing of the Protestants, do not take at all kindly to
ideas that even begin to question the unique and
supreme position of the historical Jesus. Any attempt
to marry the Vedanta to Christianity must take full
account of the fact that Christianity is a contentious
faith which requires an all-or-nothing commitment to
Jesus as the one and only incarnation of the Son of
God. Even very liberal "modernist" Christians with
doubts about the actual Godhead of Jesus will nevertheless maintain that he was "divine" in the sense of
being far-and-away the best and greatest of men.

My previous discussions did not take proper account of that whole aspect of Christianity which is
uncompromising, ornery, militant, rigorous, imperious, and invincibly self-righteous. They did not give
sufficient weight to the Church's disagreeable insistence on the reality of the totally malignant spirit of
cosmic evil, on everlasting damnation, and on the
absolute distinction between the Creator and the
creature. These thorny and objectionable facets of
Christianity cannot be shrugged off as temporary
distortions or errors. They play an essential part in
the Christian way of life, though in a manner that
must necessarily be surprising and unexpected—as I

shall try to show. Only such a uniquely "impossible" religion could be the catalyst for the remarkable developments of human consciousness and self-knowledge which distinguish Western culture since 1500. These developments are now swelling into a crisis on every level of human life—a crisis that cannot be handled unless we know, among other things, the role that Christianity has played in bringing it about.

Because this is a theme which need not require an academic approach, I have reduced bibliographical apparatus and supportive quotation from authorities to a minimum. Translations from the scriptures and liturgical texts are my own unless identified as follows: AV, the Authorized (or King James) Version; NEB, *The New English Bible;* BCP, *The Book of Common Prayer.* Loving thanks are due to my wife, Mary Jane, for expert editorial help in preparing the manuscript. I am also most grateful to Mr. Laurance Rockefeller and Harvard University, and to the Bollingen Foundation, for their generous support of a project which included work on this book.

Alan Watts

Sausalito, California
Spring, 1964

BEYOND THEOLOGY

I

The Chinese Box

Whoever *knows* that he knows must be amazed. This is both to wonder and to be lost in a maze: to wonder because knowing and being is downright weird, and to be lost in a maze because knowing that one knows generates a confusion of echoes in which the original sound is lost. For when I know that I know, which one is I? The first which knows, the second which knows that I know, or the third which knows that I know that I know?

On the one hand, to know about knowing is to think: to have in mind a formula of words or symbols which stands for the act of knowing. On the other hand, it is to turn the senses back upon themselves, to try to become physically aware of the very organs of being aware. Infants do this from the beginning: they probe, suck, and manipulate the accessible parts of their own bodies; they poke their fingers into their ears; they try touching their eyeballs; they whirl themselves around so as to feel dizzy. The only trouble is that the body is not completely accessible to itself and the senses are not fully transparent to themselves. True, I can explore someone else's body much more fully than my own, but that wasn't quite what I wanted to do: I wanted to feel it all from the inside rather than the outside.

Because, then, the senses are not fully transparent to themselves, the act of knowing (and isn't this really what I call *I*?) seems to be without any tangible foundation. It springs from the void. It stands alone: a light illumining the world, but not illumining the wires that connect it with the world, since they lie immediately behind it. I am therefore to myself a stranger in the earth, facing and meeting the world, but not really belonging.

Herein, quite simply, is the origin of man's poignant sense of individuality—of being uniquely alone, and of having an existence which is mysteriously lost and problematic. He is kicked out of Paradise, because Paradise is having a connection—roots in the garden, stem from the branch, current to the light. To be unaware of the connection is to have one's heart in the wrong place—far out in the fruit instead of within, in the tree. It is to feel that one's basic self is isolated within the body's envelope of skin, forgetting that the self is the whole circulating current from which embodiments come and go season after season, endless variations upon one theme.

A hundred gourds
from the mind
of one vine!

Nevertheless, the sensation of being lost and alone is not actually something against nature. It is a dare, an adventure, a new game of *getting* lost, as children sometimes like to be shut up in the dark. To play at being individual, alone, and afraid to die is a strangely fruitful game. Hence all wonders and myths, religion and philosophy, science and technics. Hence the whole splendid and terrible fantasy of human civilization. Hence, also, the marvelous bitter-sweetness of loving another person. Your "I" inside your skin, and my "I" inside mine, pockets of the same current, but not knowing it save in the obscure form of loving you without being able to say just why . . . I never die at all: I only get lost every time I am born, because I then come to feel that I am rolling around out there, all unconnected. And when I feel out there, I am as unconscious of my connection, of my being in fact the whole current, as I am unconscious of the brain formations which underlie consciousness.

The question to be explored is how far out can I get? How lost without being utterly lost? It is thus that when we are children, we test the limits of reality, we try to find out how much we can get away with, how far we can provoke authority without calling down wrath, and how deeply we can get involved in all sorts of games of skill without losing track. The question for the human being is how *personal* can I become without losing track? How unique? How sensitive and sympathetic? How respectful of human life, or, for that matter, of animal life? How far does my very claim to humanity depend upon protecting my own rights as against those of the collective? Even more important: is being a person in the direction of losing track? Or may it be that when the connection is lost, it can be regained only by going forward, and becoming personal to the extreme limit?

The importance of these questions lies in the fact that Western cultures have bred a type of human being who feels strongly alienated from everything which is not his own consciousness. He is a stranger both to the external world and to his own body, and in this sense he has lost his connection with the surrounding universe. He does not know that the "ultimate inside" of himself is the same as the "ultimate inside" of the cosmos, or that, in other words, his sensation of being "I" is a glimmering intimation of what the universe itself feels like on the inside. He has been taught to regard everything outside human skins as so much witless mechanism which has nothing whatsoever in common with human feelings and values. This style of man must therefore see himself as the ghastly and tragic accident of sensitive and intelligent tissue caught up in the cosmic toils like a mouse in a cotton gin.

Yet this isolated experience of identity is far out in the double sense of being very lost and very courageous: it is a heroic identity. But, alas, one of the most troublesome kinds of people is the hero without humor, who is, in this case, the style of individual who is unconscious even of the ghost of a connection. He is acting Hamlet so seriously that the player of Polonius is *actually* murdered on the stage. On the level of "real life," as well as on the level of dramatic performance, there must always remain some hint or clue (Ariadne's thread) so connecting the players with reality that they can afford to get lost in their roles. Mastery in the drama consists in so concealing the clue that it *almost* appears to be gone. So superb is the acting that the audience very nearly forgets that there is a proscenium arch, marking off the stage from actual life. Likewise, mastery in nature consists in evolving an individual organism so unique and so autonomous that it almost appears to be a separate universe. Such is human personality at its best. . . . Actually, however well concealed, the clue is always there, for if the connection were in fact to dissolve, the illusion of the separate individual would likewise vanish.

Westerners are not the only people who feel that they are disconnected individuals, out there on their own. But they *are* the only people who brag about it, and this is because the isolated style of individuality has a highly positive value in their religious and philosophical traditions. Hebrew and Greek attitudes have combined through Christianity to nurture and exaggerate this particular sensation of personal identity, and to this day both Catholic and Protestant orthodoxies stand powerfully opposed to any viewpoint that seems to compromise the "integrity" of the individual soul. Any suggestion that there is some inner level at which, as in Hinduism, God and man are identical, at which "thou art That," is dubbed *pantheism*—as if this anathema simply ended the matter then and there. To some extent this is, indeed, just as it should be, because a strongly dogmatic and authoritarian abasement of the creature—"Don't you *dare* to presume that you are God!"—is exactly what has made the Western style of individual so frisky and bumptious. He has had to exert himself mightily to achieve every kind of original, novel, and peculiarly personal success in order to justify himself before the Boss. For the Boss *notices;* he loves and judges every single creature separately, and his demands are stern. As Martin Buber once observed, in the day of judgment the Lord will not ask, "Why were you not like Moses or Elijah?" but "Why were you not like Martin Buber?" In this way the individual is ever reminded that whereas, on the one hand, he is unique and immeasurably precious in the eyes of God, on the other he has been conjured into being out of nothingness, and down to the utmost core of his existence is no more than a dependent creature. No arrangement could be more perfectly calculated to produce that particular quality of anxiety which, in the West, we believe to be the essential incentive to social and moral endeavor.

Yet today the intelligent Westerner finds himself in an odd situation which requires the deepest reconsideration of who, or what, a man is. On the one hand, it is less than a hundred years since it has seriously dawned upon Europeans and Americans that they are a minority on this planet, and that Western civilization is surrounded with peoples who are *also* civilized, but along rather different lines. Hindus and Buddhists, in particular, do not idealize the separateness of the individual, and have never felt that reality is severely divided into the spiritual and the material, the infinite and the finite, the Creator and the created. Man has not, in these other cultures, styled himself as an adopted orphan in relation to the divine.

On the other hand, man as he is described in the modern sciences has little in common with man as he feels himself subjectively. Subjectively, he remains the isolated consciousness, or soul, inhabiting a physical body. But to the biological, physical, and psychological sciences, man is a pattern of behavior in a field —like a whirlpool in water—and this behavior is ascribable equally to the bodily organism and to its environment. This *ecological* view of man as an organism/environment is as foreign to the Christian view of the embodied soul as it is to the popular materialistic view of man as an intelligent biological fluke in a mindless and mechanical world. Ecology must take the view that where the organism is intelligent, the environment also is intelligent, because the two evolve in complexity together and make up a single unified field of behavior.

However, the way in which men *feel* their existence subjectively is still very largely determined by theological and mythological images. Greek, Hebrew, and Christian images of man lie at the root of our social institutions—in our laws and the methods of enforcing them, our family structures and the raising of children, our status games, our educational and academic procedures, and, perhaps most important of all, in the very grammar of our languages. The *some-one*, the unique and specific ego, who knows and feels, who responsibly causes actions, who dwells *in* the body but is not quite *of* the body, who confronts its experiences as something other, who is the inward controller of thinking and willing—*this* is assumed in every phase of our culture and in all the practical matters of everyday life.

It matters not whether any given individual be a Christian or a Jew, a fundamentalist or an atheist: his sense of identity is nonetheless based upon a theological image. Theological images remain immensely powerful even when churches are unattended and Bibles unread. For the sensation of one's identity is not something biological, like the response of the eyes to color. It is a result of social conditioning and is itself a social institution. The child comes to feel who he is in response to the words, attitudes, and gestures of others toward him; he is defined by his social environment in the process of learning the rules of the game which his particular society is playing.[1] In turn, the rules of the social game are based historically upon traditional ideas of cosmology, and of the inner meaning of birth and death, fortune and misfortune. For this reason, then, a serious study of theology is still of immense importance in Western culture—but not in the spirit of theological seminaries, and still less in the spirit of mere historical curiosity.

What we need is a new kind of theological critique —not a polemic, not a debunking, not even a "restatement in contemporary terms." We need a natural history of theology, wherein the development of religious ideas and practices is studied, not as something good for life or bad for it, but as a form of life itself, like a particular species of flower or bird. At first sight it may seem that no approach could be more insulting than this to the true believer. For he de-

[1] This has been discussed quite fully in Ch. II of my *Psychotherapy East and West*. Pantheon Books. New York, 1961.

mands above all to be taken seriously, to know whether we are with him or against him. To such a person it is subtly but devastatingly irritating to have the discussion moved to an altogether different level, as, for example, to go into the problem of why he personally wants a firm agreement or disagreement with his point of view. This is likewise the familiar psychoanalytic gambit of "bugging" someone who wants to argue the pros and cons of two football teams, by diverting the discussion to the reason for his interest in balls. An archbishop of Dublin is reported to have said of the Church, "You may persecute us; we are quite used to that. You may argue with us and attack us; we know very well how to handle ourselves. But the one thing we will *not* tolerate is that you should explain us."

However, I have no intention to insult. On the contrary, in the perspective I am taking, the Christian tradition has appeared to me as something far, far more remarkable than I have hitherto suspected. More remarkable than it can be seen when taken, believingly, from the standpoint of orthodoxy.

The approach I am trying to follow is so simple that I am astonished that it has not been used before. And, as often happens, an unfamiliar approach is difficult to define.

As already intimated, we are going to look at Christianity simply as a phenomenon of life—like a rose bush—without asking, for the moment, whether it be true or false. Thus far the work is one of observation rather than critique or clarification. But a rose bush grows in a field or garden, and *what* the rose bush is doing can be described fully and adequately only if we see it in relation to what other plants are doing, as well as the birds, snails, greenfly, squirrels, and people. Obviously, then, the critique of theology that we need—perhaps we might call it a metatheology— must include the resources of "comparative religion." Since the close of the past century, Christian intelligentsia have woken up to find themselves in a new world—no longer the narrow domain of cultures surrounding the Mediterranean Sea, but a world in which Africa, Asia, Australasia, and the Americas are unavoidable neighbors.[2] As the context of a word may change its meaning without altering its form, so also may the context of a culture or a religion. Christianity is one thing in the context of Mediterranean and European culture, of Judaism and Islam. But in the context of Taoism and Confucianism, Hinduism and Buddhism, it may be quite another.

There is, of course, no satisfactory way of arguing the merits of any one of the great world religions against the others. In all such debates the judge and the advocate are the same person, for a man judges his own religion the best simply because the standard he uses is that of his own religious upbringing. Almost all apologies for the superiority of one religion over others come down to this tediously circular argument. I have been trying, therefore, to find a more fruitful way of making these comparisons—something that also goes much further than the mere observation that Christians do it this way, whereas Muslims do it that. The whole point of making these com-

---

[2] I am speaking, of course, of the indigenous populations of these continents, since an effective knowledge of their cultures did not become available until long after their colonization.

parisons, whether of religions or of cultures, is that the differing traditions should throw light on each other. A Christian should study Buddhism so as to get a deeper comprehension of Christianity.

"Comparative religion" or "comparative theology" has hitherto been a strictly academic pursuit, and the better authorities on the subject have been competent scholars and subtle philosophers. To date they have done such an excellent job that no one can make crass or odious comparisons between religions without making it very clear that he is an ignoramus. To say, for example, that whereas Christians believe the Ultimate Reality to be a loving, personal deity, Buddhists maintain that it is only an empty void, is to show that one understands neither Christianity nor Buddhism. For as we go into the depths of these matters, making full allowance for cultural variations, for differences of language and metaphor, and for all the semantic confusions which they engender, it appears that men's experiences of "the ultimate" are peculiarly alike. When they get down to negative or apophatic theology—the approach to God by the sculptural method of cutting away concepts—St. Dionysius and St. Thomas are speaking the same language as Nagarjuna and Shankara. At such levels the differences between sophisticated Christian theologians and Hindu or Buddhist pandits are mere technicalities. . . . But there are other levels.

The difficulty with philosophical theology is that it becomes so subtle and so abstract that it neglects the *mythic* aspect of religion. I am, of course, using the word "myth" in a special and technical sense, quite different from the vulgar usage wherein myth is falsehood, superstition, or baseless fantasy. The mythic aspect of religion is that which involves imagery or narrative, and, secondarily, participation in rituals and sacraments. Can one deny that this is by far the most effective aspect of religion so far as the vast majority of people are concerned? For images are far more moving than abstract concepts, though it is important to remember that even the most attenuated concept is still basically an image.

> It is arguable [wrote Evelyn Underhill] that every approach of the conditional mind to the Absolute God must take place by symbolic means; though these may not be of a material kind, and may even be unrecognized by those who use them. With the growth of spirituality these mediating symbols tend to become more abstract; but this does not mean that they are left behind. The "emptiness," the "darkness," the "nothing," the "Cloud of Unknowing" of the mystic, though they be negative statements, are still symbols drawn from his sensible experience, in and through which he seeks to actualize his obscure experience of God. (1)

The one respect in which Christianity differs quite essentially from other religions is in the mythic aspect, since a Christian is one who commits himself to the idea (though he will say the *fact*) that Jesus Christ was the historical incarnation of God, and that his miraculous birth, his crucifixion and resurrection, were real events which radically changed the relationship of the universe to its Creator. To say that these events are mythic is not to deny that they may also be historical, for no orthodox Christian would want to assert that they are *merely* historical, like the

Battle of Hastings or Mr. Lincoln's speaking at Gettysburg.

An approach to comparative theology which is mutually enriching in the fullest way must therefore deal with religions on the mythic level as well as the metaphysical and philosophical. But this does not mean simply the academician's comparative mythology, with its stress on the anthropological, archaeological, and literary investigation of myths. The constructive and creative "metatheologian" must be something much more than a museum curator or accomplished academic drudge. He must be a poet, not just a versifier, but a master of images—a parabolist, allegorist, analogist, and imaginator. He must be the poet in the primordial sense of the word *poiesis, poiein*—to make-do, to create. Only with this kind of imaginative handling will the myths fructify one another.

But things do not fructify one another by mere juxtaposition; they have to be woven together in some kind of active relationship, and for this purpose I have found the contextual, or Chinese box, method extraordinarily effective. For example, the holy scriptures of the Hebrews are included in those of the Christians, and, in this context, given an interpretation which the Hebrews find impossible to swallow. Nevertheless, there is nothing positively asserted in the Hebrew religion—as a matter of belief about the universe and man—which cannot be included in Christianity. Contrariwise, however, the positive assertions of Christianity cannot be encompassed by Judaism. It is simply not acceptable to the Jew that Jesus was the Lord God in the flesh. Yet Christians have no qualms about reading the Old Testament, as *they* call it, as a collection of inspired writings which forebode the coming of Christ.

The fact that the Christian scriptures can include the Hebrew, but not the Hebrew the Christian, does not imply that Christianity is a better or truer religion than Judaism. From the standpoint of an unprejudiced observer, it implies only that if you put the Hebrew revelation within the context of the Christian revelation, the former undergoes a most interesting transformation. Whether or not this transformation will be something more than interesting, that is, deeply moving and convincing, will depend upon the reaction of each individual.

Now, some of the great Catholic missionaries to India, such as the Jesuit Robert de Nobili, have suggested that the Hindu scriptures—notably the *Upanishads* and the *Bhagavad-Gita*—should be regarded as a supplementary Old Testament. The notion is laudable, but will it work? Does Hinduism assert anything positively that cannot be included within Christianity? Alas, there is in Hinduism the crucial doctrine of *tat tvam asi* ("That art thou"), which asserts the ultimate identity of oneself and the Godhead. At the level of philosophical theology we can probably iron this difference out. We can doubtless argue that the "self" referred to here is not the ego, not the personal soul (the Hebrew *nefesh*), but the spirit, the *ruach Adonai* or breath of the Lord which gave life to the clay image of Adam when it was breathed into its nostrils. We might say that the ground of man's being is the immanent presence of God, which at every moment supports and energizes both soul and body—a "beyond" which is "within." As one of the Christian mystics put it, "He is thy being, but thou art not his."

But this is a subtlety which takes the whole excitement out of the issue. At the mythic level, Hinduism asserts that all experience whatsoever is God's, and that God is the one and only knower and seer. All multiplicity, all sensations of limited and separate individuality, of the duality of here and there, I and thou, are God's dream or *maya*—a word that signifies not only illusion but also art and miraculous power. The universe is therefore conceived as God's game (*lila*) of hide-and-seek with himself, such that all beings are simply the masks of the one divine Self (*atman*).[3]

This is an essentially dramatic view of the cosmos, contrasting sharply with the Hebrew and Christian view of the world as an artifact. In the former, the creature is the role or disguise of the Creator, but in the latter the creature is as distinct from the Creator as the table from the carpenter. But from the Christian standpoint the former view is quite inadmissible, quite shockingly blasphemous. (The Jews felt the same about the divine claims of Jesus.) For one of the major values of Christianity, as of all strictly theistic religions, is the eternal importance of *differences*. Christianity therefore insists vehemently on an absolutely essential difference between the Creator and the creature, between good and evil, and between

[3] Some Hindu pandits, especially of the extreme *advaita*, or non-dualist, school, may accuse me of using very loose language here, but I must repeat that I am speaking mythically, not metaphysically, that is, of the *saguna* and not the *nirguna* Brahman.

one creature and another. It has often struck me that Christian preachers and apologists like to assume a nubbly or prickly attitude when discussing these matters, coming out in the clipped and crusty tone of their voices.

> How unpleasant to meet Mr. Eliot!
> With his features of clerical cut,
> And his brow so grim
> And his mouth so prim
> And his conversation, so nicely
> Restricted to What Precisely
> And If and Perhaps and But. (2)

And, of course, What Precisely is very, very important. One really needs to know whether the transparent stuff in the bottle is gin or muriatic acid.

Christianity even brings the principle of differentiation into the Godhead itself with the doctrine of the Trinity, insisting, vehemently as ever, that the Father is not the Son, and the Son is not the Holy Spirit, but that nonetheless all three are one and the same God. It objects to what it calls the "monism" of the Hindus because, without differentiation, there is no place for the supreme values of love and relationship. However, this argument cuts both ways because what the Christian says about the "Three in One and One in Three" relationship of the Trinity is almost exactly what the Hindu says about the "Many in One and One in Many" arrangement of the universe. If the latter makes love between the members unreal, so does the former.

If, then, the Christian system cannot contain the Hindu, can the Hindu contain the Christian? Hindus are, of course, notoriously tolerant, and it is well known that Sri Ramakrishna lived for some time as a Christian in order to complete his understanding of the many aspects of divine revelation. But wouldn't the Christian say that Sri Ramakrishna could not really have become a Christian without committing himself to the sole and exclusive role of Jesus Christ as the savior of the world? And wouldn't he also have had to renounce the proud blasphemy of "I am That?"

To understand this we must go rather more deeply into what was presumably Sri Ramakrishna's attitude, so as to understand the special kind of respect which a Hindu might have for the Christian viewpoint. When the Hindu says that the universe is God's *maya* or dream, the word *maya* is not necessarily used in a bad sense, as if it were a *mere* dream. I have said that *maya* also means art and miraculous power, the creation of an illusion so fabulous that it takes in its Creator. God himself is literally a-mazed at and in his own work. Were it otherwise, it would certainly be no fun to be God. But a-mazement means, among other things, getting deliberately lost, and this would naturally involve God's finding himself in a position where he seems not to be God at all, but merely a creature. Getting still further lost, he might well find himself in the most critical of all possible situations: confronted with the ultimate gamble—the necessity of making an immediate choice between everlasting bliss and everlasting torment, without being quite sure how to choose. Will you take what is in the right hand, or the left? Choose the right one!

Without any disrespect it must be said that Christianity is preeminently the gambler's religion. In no other religion are the stakes so high and the choice so momentous. Nowhere else is the good so gracious and the evil so blackly malignant. From the Hindu's point of view, then, the Christian's predicament is the extreme adventure of God into his own *maya*. The Hindu must gape at it as we look at trapeze artists and tightrope walkers in the circus, and what can he do but applaud? The ultimate act: the juggler, scared out of his own wits, keeping six bottles of nitroglycerin whirling from hand to hand. But in this case the bottles are the stars and galaxies.

The first and quite natural reaction of an orthodox Christian to this point of view is that it deprives the differences between God and man, good and evil, of ultimate reality. If they are no more than a temporary *maya*, they are not truly important at all. But that is a most improper thing for a Christian to say, for it is to assert the essential unimportance of whatever is temporal and finite, including, among other things, *history*. For it is the very center of Christian faith that the world has been redeemed by a temporal and historical event, the crucifixion of Jesus Christ under Pontius Pilate, somewhere around 30 A.D. This event began and ended in time, and, according to the story, culminated in a resurrection from death which must have been as shockingly splendid as any other awakening from a hideous nightmare. This event is past, gone, vanished, as surely as if it had been a film of smoke in the air. But will any Christian say that it was for this reason unimportant and unreal?

According to the Hindu myth, the supreme Self is always going in and out of time, so that the *maya* is at once temporal and ever-returning. For a *kalpa* or "day of Brahma" lasting 4,320,000 years, the world of *maya* is manifested, and then for another *kalpa* comes the night, the *pralaya* in which the illusion is withdrawn, and in which the Godhead recollects its own nature, free from space, time, and finitude. But thereafter the illusion begins again, and the days and nights of Brahma continue forever and ever. From the most deeply metaphysical and esoteric point of view, these days and nights must be regarded as simultaneous, as aspects of an eternal present which is "nowever." Rightly understood, a single instant is as long as a century of *kalpas,* and all time is in just one pulse of come/go.

We are saying, then, that differences are no less important for being relative or temporal differences. When one comes to think of it, a permanent or eternal difference would be something as monstrous as an infinitely tall man. Do those Christians who affirm the eternal distinction of Creator and creature, and the everlasting persistence of heaven and hell without rhythm or relief, actually pause to consider what they are saying? Any scholar of the Bible should realize that its language is often poetic and metaphorical, and to say that the blessed shall rejoice and the damned shall be tormented "forever" refers not to chronological measure but to the degree of intensity of an experience. When people said, "O king, live forever!" they did not intend it literally, but when the interpretation of the Bible got into the hands of (Roman) lawyers instead of poets, this kind of thoughtless literalism became dogma. If, however, the Christian imagery is set within the context of the Hindu, the razor-edge path between salvation and damnation, with all the magnificent and appalling consequences that this illusion has had for mankind, becomes one of the greatest *dramatic* situations of all time.

But once this is said, once the show has been given away, hasn't all the magic of Christianity been dispelled? Instead of being a context for the Christian view, wouldn't the Hindu viewpoint simply swallow it up? The answer to that problem must unfold itself through the course of this book. But in the meantime, there is simply this consideration: is anyone *absolutely* sure that the world is *maya,* that he himself is —deep down—the dreaming Godhead, that death is a change of scene, and that the choice between endless glory and endless horror is just a device for making things thrilling? Isn't it just possible that such ideas as these may be the most insidious hallucinations, the most persuasive and corrupting temptations of that arch-fiend and enemy of creation, the Devil? No one—not even, I think, the Godhead—is absolutely sure. For to be is courage, and to know is nerve. The answer is always "Yes/No," because existence itself is a vibratory or wavelike affair, a "now-you-see-it-now-you-don't," a back/front, up/down, here/ there situation like a mountain or wave with its up side and its down side, clearly different from each other and yet inseparable.

To be *quite* sure, to be set, fixed, and firm is to miss the point of life. For living and being is a perpetual abandonment of the known and fixed situation. The only true peace is the always slightly uncertain apprehension that No will imply Yes, just as much as Yes implies No. Hence the following is my favorite quotation from Shankara, the St. Thomas of the Hindus:

> Now a distinct and definite knowledge is possible in respect of everything capable of becoming an object of knowledge: but it is not possible in the case of That which cannot become such an object. That is Brahman, for It is the Knower, and the Knower can know other things, but cannot make Itself the object of Its own knowledge, in the same way that fire can burn other things but cannot burn itself. Neither can it be said that Brahman is able to become an object of knowledge for anything other than Itself, since outside Itself there is nothing which can possess knowledge. (3)

In other words, the root and ground, the "firm foundation," of the universe has nothing to stand upon, not even itself. It has no knowledge of the "how" of its own inner workings. This is no defect for the simple reason that this knowledge is not necessary. Light has no need to shine upon itself. But when we, who are used to leaning upon something, first get into touch with this inmost dimension of ourselves, it feels as if nothing is there, as if, in Ruysbroeck's words, our whole life is "grounded upon an abyss."

There is, then, a fascinating contrast between the popular and mythic conception of the Hindu and of the Christian God. The latter is associated with the potter and the carpenter. He is the supreme technician who knows just how everything is done, who can explain everything, and who comprehends, through and through, the mystery of his own being. He knows all the answers. When I was a child and was asking my mother impossible questions about the why and wherefore of life and death, she would often say that there are some things we are just not meant to know —at any rate for the time being. However, after we had died and gone to heaven, God would make everything clear. So I used to think that on wet afternoons in heaven everyone would gather around the Throne of Grace and ask Omniscience "Why did you do this?" and "How did you do that?" and that the Lord would patiently and kindly give completely satisfactory answers.

"Father, why are the leaves green?"

"Because of the chlorophyll."

"Oh."

The Hindu God is shown, not as a technician, but as a being with many arms and many faces, a cosmic centipede of fantastic dexterity moving innumerable limbs without, however, having to *think* about it, to know how it is done. In just the same way, we move our own arms and legs, beat our hearts, shape our bones, constellate our nervous systems, and grow our hair with astounding efficiency and yet without needing to explain it. Indeed, thinking about these processes often interferes with them, just as the actor or dancer falters when he is too conscious of himself.

Therefore if anyone brought up in a Christian culture says, "I am God," we conclude at once that he is insane, but humor him by asking technical questions. "How did you create the world in six days?" "Why did you allow the Devil to get into the Garden of Eden?" "What were you doing before you created the universe?" But, in India, when someone suddenly declares, "I am God," they say, "Congratulations! At last you found out." For them, the claim to be God does not involve the claim to encyclopedic omniscience and completely arbitrary omnipotence. The reason is that they know very well what a completely omniscient and omnipotent being would do. Imagine a world in which all the ambitions of technology have been fulfilled, where everyone has a panel of push-buttons which, at the lightest touch, will satisfy every desire more swiftly than the djinn of Aladdin's lamp. Less than five minutes after this ambition has been attained, it will be essential to include upon the panel a button marked SURPRISE! For Hindus, the world-as-it-is is the result of having pushed that button; it is terrifyingly magical—at once far, far out of control yet at the same time one's own inmost will.

What we mean, in the Western world, by knowing how things are done is that we can describe the process in words, or some other form of symbolism. It is thus that our education consists almost entirely of learning skill with symbols—reading, writing, and arithmetic—relegating skill in kinesthetic, social, and esthetic matters to extracurricular activities. But the conduct and regulation of the whole human organism, not to mention the whole universe, is manifestly an affair so swift and so complex that no lumbering string of words can account for it. The omniscience of God is precisely that he does not have to think before he acts. He knows how to produce the universe just as I know how to breathe.

In sum, then, I would say that a "metatheology" should have at least three basic operating principles. The first is that we look at a religion, not as something *about* life, but as a form of life, a way of life, as genuine and authentic as a rose bush or a rhinoceros. For a living religion is not a commentary on existence: it is a kind of existing, an involvement, a participation.

The second is the Chinese box or contextual principle, whereby we illumine one theological system (in this case the Christian) by looking at it and seeing what happens to it in the context of another. This is the same sort of procedure as studying Chinese culture to get a better understanding of the basic institutions of our own culture; for a culture emerged in China that was very highly sophisticated and yet, in several respects, as unlike our own as anything on earth. It therefore offers the most admirable opportunity for instructive comparisons. Christians are characteristically leery of such procedures, but should take comfort from the fact that Hinduism is not a competitive or proselytizing organization like the Roman Catholic or United Presbyterian Churches. There is no head office to write to, and therefore no society out to "get" you and score you as a member.

The third—a rather radical departure from the methods of scholarly theologians—is to deal with the subject almost naïvely, at its mythic, imagistic, or anthropomorphic level. I have found that this has many advantages, the most important of which is that it avoids the danger of idolatry. No educated person can take the anthropomorphic image of God quite seriously, and therefore, when he uses it, he knows he is using an image and does not mistake it for the reality. On the other hand, a highly refined abstraction looks as if it isn't an image, and is thus much more easily confused with a direct description of "the

Truth." We should never forget that all our ideas of the universe, whether theological, metaphysical, or scientific, are anthropomorphic—being translations of the way things are into the terminology of the human brain. Thus to think of God as Necessary Being or as the organic Pattern of the Universe can be much closer to idolatry than thinking of him as the Old Gentleman upon the golden throne, or as the many-armed and many-faced Dancer who is playing as the world. Another advantage of this imagery is that it enables us to discuss theological problems in a lively and dramatic way that is intelligible to people at many different levels of intelligence, and of many different *kinds* of intelligence.

Hitherto, Christian theologians have, on the whole, been rather ashamed of their imagery. Since Clement and Origen first tried to make Christianity look respectable in the eyes of Greek intellectuals, theologians have bent over backwards to assure us that heaven is not literally up in the sky, that angels don't really go around in white nighties, and that God the Holy Ghost is not actually a dove.[4] By now they have made their point, and thus we can safely return to rich and colorful imageries, and to churches and temples radiant with figures of gods, saints, and angels.

[4] Martin Luther twitted the Archbishop of Mainz as having, among his collection of holy relics, two feathers and an egg from the Holy Ghost as a dove.

II

Is It Serious?

The most profound metaphysical questions are expressed in the most common phrases of everyday life. Who do you think *you* are? Who started this? Are we going to make it? Where are we going to put it? Who's going to clean up? Where the hell d'you think you're going? Where do *I* come in? What's the time? Where am I? What's up? Which is which? Who's who? Do you mean it? Where do we get off? Are you there? But there seems to be one that must be asked right at the beginning. Is it serious?

The most remarkable superficial difference between Christianity and Hinduism is that the former replies "Yes" and the latter "No." The King of kings and the Lord of lords very definitely expects to be

taken seriously. Thunders and lightnings proceed
from his throne, and, quite aside from any of the very
serious demands that are made for moral behavior
between man and man, the Ruler of Heaven requires
above all that he be worshiped, and his faithful congregation responds with the words of the psalm, "O
come let us worship and fall down, and kneel before
the Lord our maker!"

When I was a schoolboy, we were dragooned into
attending the services at Canterbury Cathedral, the
Mecca of the Anglican Church. As we knelt, bowed,
or stood in the courtly and austere ceremonies of this
ancient fane, we had to take the utmost care never
to laugh or smile—an offense punishable with ruth-
less floggings, and very difficult to avoid because of
the astonishing idiosyncrasies of the venerable clergy,
with their propensities for bleating, whining, or bum-
bulating the prayers in sundry varieties of holy-
sounding voices. There were rumbling Pooh-bahs,
and wizened little ascetics preaching with fervent
shrieks, and between stands in pulpit or lectern they
would process hither and yon, attired so as to look
like rows of well-ordered penguins. . . . And yet
neither the deadly seriousness of our postures nor the
pathetic comedy of the clerics could quite conceal
the atmosphere of luminous glory. High and echoing
spaces of pale gray stone, enchanted with light that
fell through the most intricate stained glass, predomi-
nantly blue; stone smelling faintly and pleasantly
musty, like a wine cellar, and the whole building
seeming to float above the congregation with the dignity and independence of a gull in the sky. Floating
above the then grubby little city of Canterbury, so

that its arches and spires belonged elsewhere, perhaps upon some high and inaccessible cliffs to the far West, overlooking the Atlantic, where angels still kept guard over the Holy Grail.

I revive these memories to suggest that the sense of divine royalty is not altogether demanding and imperious, and that therefore the worship of the King of kings, dwelling in inaccessible light, is not necessarily a cringing obedience or a stern duty. It may also have the sense of immense celebration, a strong-swinging, statelily lilting dance of total joy. The *Gloria in excelsis* sung at Easter, with the bells ringing wild. The golden splendor of the Greek or Russian liturgy, where people do not kneel, but stand or wander freely in a domed temple that is deliberately made to suggest the glory of heaven. More and more one gets the impression that the object of this worship is no pompous prince, but something like living light, which is all at once as sympathetic as the fire on your hearth and as blasting as the explosion of a star. And as full of delight as a diamond in the sun. As the Catholic poet Coventry Patmore put it: "If we may credit certain hints contained in the lives of the saints, love raises the spirit above the sphere of reverence and worship into one of laughter and dalliance: a sphere in which the soul says:

> Shall I, a gnat which dances in Thy ray,
> *Dare* to be reverent?"

Yet it must be admitted that in the Christian climate of the English-speaking world, such penetrations of the façade are rare. The insides of most Protestant churches resemble courthouses or town halls, and the focal point of their services is a serious exhortation from a man in a black gown. No golden light, no bells, incense, and candles. No mystery upon an altar or behind an iconostasis. But people brought up in this atmosphere seem to love it. It feels warm and folksy, and leads, on the one hand, to hospitals, prison reform, and votes for all, and, on the other, to sheer genius for drabness, plain cooking ungraced with wine, and constipation of the bright emotions— all of which are considered virtues. If I try to set aside the innate prejudices which I feel against this religion, I begin to marvel at the depth of its commitment to earnestness and ugliness. For there is a point at which certain types of ugliness become fascinating, where one feels drawn to going over them again and again, much as the tongue keeps fondling a hole in a tooth. I begin to realize that those incredibly plain people, with their almost unique lack of color, may after all be one of the most astonishing reaches of the divine *maya*—the Dancer of the world as far out from himself as he can get, dancing not-dancing.

For them, as for many other Christians and Jews of all shades of belief, the Lord is an archetypal grandfather, who, because it is necessary to conceive him in the human image, has a fault which, in a human being, is insufferable: he has never done anything wrong, or, if he has, he absolutely refuses to admit it. The same is true of the usual conception of Jesus. The minister's son who won't go behind the fence with the other boys for a peeing contest. So they throw him in the pond, but instead of fighting back he takes on a nobly injured attitude to make them feel guilty. But then, the most tough and ancient theological problem is the "mystery of iniquity" —not how the universe came into being, but how the snake got into the garden, how evil arose in a creation ruled omnipotently by one who is so perfectly good.

The big question is whether there is actually a twinkle in the Father's eye; whether, before the creation began and there was no one around as a witness, there was not a special arrangement between the Lord and the Devil, a conspiracy such that the whole drama of the cosmos depends upon its being kept (almost) secret. For if the Lord is *absolutely* serious, things are very bad. Not only does he confront his creatures with severe moral demands; he also fits them out with lusty, hungry, and highly sensitive bodies liable to cancer, bubonic plague, arthritis, decayed teeth, and stomach ulcers; he flings them into a world containing mosquitoes, sharks, tapeworms, piranha fish, staphylococci, and other people; he puts them into a situation in which it has, on the whole, required considerable effort not to get involved in tortures and burnings, whether judicial or accidental, in wars, murders, and robberies, and in the weird emotional tangles that come from having a brain which finds it a necessary advantage to predict a (mostly) dreaded future. On top of this, he is alleged to threaten those who disobey his commandments with the most exquisitely painful tortures ever devised, to endure for always and always without rest.

Of course there are temporary compensations, but the contemplation of this frightful panorama of possibilities and certainties is what is called "facing reality." It is at once very irreverent and yet absolutely necessary to call this façade in question. Is God quite serious? To put it in another way: is this a universe in which there is the possibility of a total and irremediable disaster, of everlasting damnation or some equivalent thereof? Or is it a universe in which to be or not to be is *not* the question, since the one endlessly implies the other?

In the imagery of Hinduism the hard reality of the world confronting us is, as we have seen, *lila* (play) and *maya* (magical illusion). Shiva dances the universe, surrounded with flames and flashing terrors, but one of his many hands is held upright with palm open to the spectator. The meaning is "Fear not." This performance is a big act. The solidity of the rocks is an electrical mirage. The body is a whirlpool, constant only in appearance, but actually a stream of changes. And pain, the very touchstone of reality, since we pinch ourselves to be sure that we are not dreaming, is a hypnotic state which can be switched on or off at will.

There is obviously no objective test that can be applied here. I can find out whether the world is serious or not only by personal experiment, that is, if the answer can be found at all. I may take the Lord God at his word, stop asking impertinent questions, and prostrate myself at the foot of the Throne. Or I may gently call his bluff and wait—poker-faced, trembling, or eagerly confident. It may well be that the Lord will play with me to the final microsecond of the last moment—perhaps with a long and terrible silence, perhaps with all the plagues and pains of the flesh, perhaps with visitations from subtly convincing prophets and preachers, and doubtless, at the very end. with the kindly priest and his Last Rites. On the surface, it will seem that I am just resisting divine authority, that I am refusing to let Love into my heart, that I am proudly repressing that inner voice of the terrified conscience, urging me to melt and run weeping and screaming to Heaven in sorrow for my sins. But if there is a man of such spiritual courage as to call the Lord's bluff, what he is actually refusing to believe, what he will not take seriously, is not the Lord but his *maya*. He will not admit that agony and tragedy, that death and hell, fear and nothingness, are ultimate realities. Above all, he is not admitting the final reality of separateness, of the seeming distinction between man and cosmos, creature and Creator.

To the orthodox this courage will seem blasphemous, and to the skeptical and secular-minded it will seem to be wishful, since such persons have a view of reality that is grimmer by far than even Jonathan Edwards' conception of the Angry God. For the secularist imagines the universe beyond and outside man to be essentially dead, mechanical, and stupid. With him it is high dogma that nature cares nothing for human values, but is a system of confusion which produced us by mere chance, and therefore must be beaten down and made to submit to man's will. Now, there is something in this view of the universe which is akin to states of consciousness found in psychosis. The vision of the world as a Malicious System which eggs you on with hopes, just to keep you alive, and then grinds you horribly to bits. In this state there is no luminosity in things. Faces, flowers, waters, and hills all look as though they were made of plastic or enameled tin—the whole scene a tick-tock toy shop, a nightmare of metal and patent leather, garish under reflected light alone. Other people aren't really alive; they're mocked-up mannequins, automatic responders pretending to be alive. Even oneself is a self-frustrating mechanism in which every gain in awareness is balanced by new knowledge of one's ridiculous and humiliating limitations.

Those who, outside mental hospitals, like to see things this way persuade themselves and others that this attitude is somehow not only realistic but heroic. In philosophical arguments they can always one-up the religious or metaphysically inclined by a show of being down-to-earth and hard-boiled. Perhaps it is just a matter of temperament that some people simply cannot take that view of things; for me it has always seemed peculiarly odd that there is anything at all. It would have been so much easier and so much less effort for there *not* to have been any universe, that I find it impossible to think that the game is not worth the candle. A cosmos that was not basically an expression of joy and bliss would surely have found some way of committing suicide almost at the beginning, for there is not the least point in surviving compulsively.

One should not be ashamed of wishful thinking, for this is just what all inventive and creative people do. They are dreamers, and they find ways of realizing their dreams because they wish and dream effectively. That is to say, their wishful thinking is not vague; their desires are imagined so precisely and specifically that they can very often be carried out. The trouble with many religions, accused of wishful thinking, is that they are not wishful enough. They show a deplorable lack of imagination and of adventure in trying to find out what it is that one really wants. I cannot conceive any better way of trying to understand myself, or human nature in general, than a thorough exploration of my desires, making them as specific as possible, and then asking myself whether that is *actually* what I want.

What, then, if I were to construct a religion as a pure work of art, creating a picture of the universe as wishful as it could possibly be? On the one hand, such a construction would be the purest play and fantasy, wholly lacking in seriousness. But on the other hand, fantasies are sometimes unexpectedly productive. The strictly playful and speculative constructions of mathematicians often turn out to be useful formulae for understanding the physical world. For the pure mathematician is much more of an artist than a scientist. He does not simply measure the world. He invents complex and playful patterns without the least regard for their practical applicability. He might almost be on a permanent vacation—as if he were sitting on the terrace of a seaside hotel, doing crossword puzzles and playing chess or poker with his cronies. But he works in a university, which makes it respectable, and his games and puzzles are marvels of intricacy. When Riemann had invented equations, not merely for 4-dimensional spaces, but for 5, 6, 7, and n-dimensional spaces, it was found that these equations could be applied to problems in price fluctuation!

The historian, too, is basically an artist, selecting from the infinitude of past events those that will fit into some significant and intelligible pattern, for his art is to *make sense* of human doings. Likewise the Copernican theory of the solar system is preferable to the Ptolemaic mainly because it is simpler. The planets do not have to backtrack in their courses, but proceed smoothly upon their orbits. The picture is cleaner and tidier, and thus more satisfactory from an *esthetic* point of view.

Why not ask, therefore, what might be the most esthetically satisfying explanation for one's own existence in our particular universe? It must be an explanation that will completely satisfy me for the most appalling agonies that can be suffered in this world. Upon what terms would I be actually *willing* to endure them?

We will often suffer willingly to help those we love, and it is along these lines that Christian theology has generally tried to justify suffering. Pain is transformed by offering it to God as an act of adoration. There is no greater love than to lay down one's life for a friend, and this is finally what God himself is always doing. This is the sacrifice of God the Son, offered because "God so loved the world." To Christians, the meaning of suffering is therefore that it evokes love and gives reality to love. The love which God bears toward the world is real because, in some way, it is *costing*—even to God. As the hymn says:

> There was no other good enough
> To pay the price of sin;
> He only could unlock the gates
> Of heaven, and let us in.

Yet though I may be willing to suffer for those I love, I am not willing that *they* should suffer. Indeed,

I will my suffering for them just because I do *not* will theirs. A universe in which my friends have to suffer is thoroughly objectionable if their only compensation is that it evokes my love for them, or even if it evokes God's love. From our standpoint of wishful thinking, a universe in which suffering happens by mistake is just badly made, and a universe in which suffering comes upon us through the malice of someone else is a diabolical trap. Ideally, I would want to be solely responsible for my own suffering, including my own painful feelings about the suffering of others. I would wish the same privilege for everyone else. But obviously this must mean something much more than responsibility in its ordinary sense, for it has to include the case of the baby born with syphilis.

Popular Hinduism and Buddhism explain such tragedies as the individual's *karma*, his own doing, inherited from a former life. The syphilitic baby is therefore paying a price for some evil that he has done in a previous incarnation. But this is not so much an explanation as an indefinite postponement of explanation. Why and how does the reincarnating individual *first* go wrong? Responsibility for one's own suffering cannot be attributed to the individual as we know and see him superficially, for, at this level, the individual—whether adult or infant—seems far more the victim than the agent of his agony.

We must therefore imagine a new kind of individuality in which there are two spheres with a common center. The outer sphere is the finite consciousness, the ego, the superficial individual, which believes itself to be the willing agent and knower, or the passive sufferer, of deeds and experience. But the inner sphere is the real self, unknown to the conscious ego. For the latter is the temporary disguise or dream of the former, and the real Self would not only be unafraid of entering into dreams of intense suffering; it would all the time be experiencing the process as delight and bliss, as an eternal game of hide-and-seek.

This fantasy religion would then require the final condition that at some time the two spheres would merge, that my inmost Self would awaken from its dream to transform my superficial ego with a shock of recognition. Perhaps this is why we sometimes have a strangely pleasant sensation of having forgotten something extremely important from long, long ago. Occasionally, this shadow of a memory comes with hints of a forgotten paradise, some luminous landscape of hills and waters which is utterly familiar and yet completely unidentifiable. Every now and then the "real" world reminds us of it, and we think, "This is what I have always been looking for. This place feels like home." At other times, the memory has a much deeper dimension—a sensation of being immeasurably ancient and knowing, as somehow prior to time and space. But there is nothing at all specific about it, for though the sensation is vivid, it is tantalizingly ephemeral. These are, then, intimations of something to be remembered which is, as it were, a vast dimension of one's being which has been kept hidden—perhaps from the moment of birth. For consciousness, or conscious attention, is the trick of noticing the figure and ignoring the background, and in the same way I seem to notice my ego and forget my background, the larger Self which underlies my ego.

Let us suppose, then, that my overt life as an individual is being imagined by a hidden Self that is actually much more the central *me* than my ego, and that at some unspecified time (if only the moment of death) I shall wake up and recollect the infinite joy which is expressing itself in this endless game of dancing in and out of the light. Merely to define the state of the inmost Self as "infinite joy" is to dodge the real task of inventing an ideal religion. If my fantasy is to approach being a work of art, I must try to define quite clearly what I want in this transcendental joy.

Thus it should be noted, in passing, that Christian imagery is very vague about the glories of heaven and amazingly specific about the agonies of hell. Pictures of people in heaven are invariably demure and dull, whereas hell is a writhing orgy (4). Hints of heaven come in the stained glass of Sainte-Chapelle and the illuminated manuscripts of Lindisfarne, in the glowing rites of the Eastern Liturgy, and in the chanting of the Solesmes Benedictines. But these are no more than strains, heard through a door held briefly ajar. It is time to venture more boldly into the dynamics of delight to discover what we really want from heaven.[1]

[1] I am reminded of the story of a dinner-table conversation in an English country house, where the guests were discussing their ideas of what would happen to them after death. Among those present was an elderly and somewhat stuffy gentleman, who happened to be a prominent layman in the Church. He had been silent throughout the conversation, and at last the hostess turned to him and said, "Well, Sir Roderick, what do *you* think will happen to you after death?" "I am perfectly certain," he replied, "that I shall go to heaven and enjoy everlasting bliss, but I wish you wouldn't discuss such a depressing subject."

Our fantasy religion will take it for granted that the inmost Self is eternal and indestructible, simply because it is what there is and all that there is. The totality of space will be the field of its consciousness, and this will fit in very well with current astronomical ideas of space as a four-dimensional continuum curving in upon itself but having no outside. Perhaps the exploration of space is really the exploration and extension of our own consciousness, a rediscovery of the ignored background of each individual ego. But what, specifically, will the preoccupations of this consciousness be?

If work is what *must* be done in order to go on living, the proper activity of That-which-Is will obviously be play. Reality is what exists without effort, Blake's energy which is eternal delight. I have suggested that hide-and-seek, or lost-and-found, is the fundamental form of play because, at root, being is vibration. It is a state of yes/no, solid/space, here/there, positive/negative, come/go, inside/outside, symbolized in the fundamental up/down motion of the wave. Rhythm lies at the heart of play, and thus various rhythmic actions are the primordial forms of delight—birdsong, the chirping of crickets, the beating of hearts, the pulsation of laughter, the ecstatic loss of self in drumming and dancing, the sonorous vibrations of voices and strings and bells. Absorption in rhythm can go on and on until energy fails, for when we survey the various cultures of mankind it appears there is nothing men would rather do than be lost all night in rhythm. This is why the Christian angels sing "Alleluia, alleluia!" forever before the

Vision of God, and why their Buddhist counterparts are alleged to chant

> Tutte, tutte,
> Vutte, vutte,
> Patte, patte,
> Katte, kattel (5)

I am quite sure, therefore, that an essential component of my heaven and preoccupation of the inmost Self would be absorption in rhythm; and as I look at light and water and listen to the pulses in my own body, I can hardly doubt that this is the truth. There is supreme delight in flowing with an unobstructed rhythm. But it is from the obstruction of rhythmic activity that we get our sensations of matter, substance, weight, and rigidity; activity becomes unpleasant when overwhelmed by these sensations. Death seems to be the dissolution of activity into mere matter. Nevertheless, without some degree of obstruction, rhythm does not happen at all. There is no beat without the skin of the drum. Rhythm is blissful so long as the obstruction is subordinate to the action, so long as matter is repeatedly overcome by energy. To realize rhythm, the infinite consciousness will therefore have to obstruct itself in some degree, just as space must contain solids in order to be recognized as space.

A further obstacle to the delight of rhythm is monotony, which play avoids by variety and complexity. But there must be *some* monotony or regularity for there to be any rhythm or pattern at all. Otherwise we should have only a succession of random intervals. The main problem in the art of rhythm is not to abolish monotony, but always to be in the process of overcoming it anew Thus there is variety not only in the beat of rhythms but in the medium—drum, string, tube, bell, and then on to rhythm in bodily motion, in form and visual pattern, in transformations of color, in songs and poetry, and in the complexities of pure ideas. And beyond this, the dramas and plots of human history, the fortunes of war, the stratagems of love, the gambling financiers, and the endless pursuit of the illusion of political power—all these are variations and complications of delight in rhythm. Once more, delight consists in the total absorption of the mind in these patterns. The delight requires that there must always be some resistance to the play of patterned energy, and this may be monotony, the sluggishness which turns energy into effort, or just too great a degree of complexity, so that the pattern falls into chaos.

To maintain the state of bliss, the infinite consciousness must have the most ingenious ways of both having monotony and overcoming it, of so combining order with randomness that the principle of order does not issue in dead uniformity, nor the principle of randomness in chaos. The play of rhythm must be controlled, and yet not so controlled as to be completely predictable. It must be marvelously complicated, but without the tedium of having to keep track of all the ins and outs. In short, omnipotence must at all costs avoid the stultifying situation of being in total control of itself, and the equally fruitless situation of losing control altogether.

The solution is similar to the trick whereby an organism relegates certain functions to "the unconscious," so that they continue without having to be directed consciously, as for example the deliberate selection of words in speaking, or the use of the breath in swimming. This has a double advantage. On the one hand, it allows the complexity of patterns to develop without becoming burdensome to the original center of control. On the other, it introduces an element of surprise, for the inmost Self is thus enabled to let some of the patterns of its behavior go off on their own and to forget that it has done so. In some such way, the delight of our hypothetical Godhead would be maintained by introducing the experience of otherness. For these relegated, or delegated, rhythms would issue forth in the guise of other beings to the amazement of their progenitor.

Yet these "others" still remain the behavior of the inmost Self. In them, the Self therefore forgets itself. On the one hand, this is an adventure, a temporary surrender of control which prevents the over-all system of control from becoming rigid and dead. On the other hand, this forgetting is a refreshment, like sleep, since it creates standpoints from which everything can be seen anew. With every baby born, the inmost Self would look forth upon its world and be as astonished as if it had never before beheld it! In this way the unthinkably ancient universe would be renewed forever and ever, and the dance never pall.

But the sensation of otherness must not become excessive. When it becomes so, when the feeling that things are out of control reaches a certain point, surprise becomes frustration or fear and panic. At such crises, my inmost Self would have to have the power of recollecting that the whole play is its own, that otherness is *maya*. And then, in still another way, it would wake up in astonishment, but this time at its own cosmic and eternal dimensions. Yet sometimes, like a boy on a dare, it might let things go very far out of control, even to the extent of letting itself forget that it had the power to awaken. When we are asleep, or dreaming, we do not know that we can wake up. But we could not happily commit ourselves to sleep in the first place unless we knew that we could. It is in the same spirit that a sailor, confident in his skill and in his ship, commits himself to the storms. For playing is also gambling—inventing the sense of risk, and seeing how far out one can get.

This is more or less what I would do if I had the power to dream every night of anything I wanted. For some months, I would probably fulfill all the more obvious wishes. There might be palaces and banquets, players and dancing girls, fabulous bouts of love, and sunlit gardens beside lakes, with mountains beyond. There would next be long conversations with sages, contemplation of supreme works of art, hearing and playing music, voyages to foreign lands, flying out into space to see the galaxies, and delving into the atom to watch the wiggling wavicles. But the night would come when I might want to add a little spice of adventure—perhaps a dream of dangerous mountain-climbing, of rescuing a princess from a dragon, or, better, an unpredictable dream in which I do not know what will happen. Once this had started, I might get still more daring. I would wish to dream whole lifetimes, packing seventy years into a single night. I would dream that I am not dreaming at all, that I will never wake up, that I have completely lost myself somewhere down the tangled corridors of the mind, and, finally, that I am in such excruciating agony that when I wake up, it will be better than all possible dreams.

By now it will be obvious that my hidden Self could very well be imagining just this particular situation and personality in which I now find myself. The same would be true for every other individual, for in our hypothesis the inmost Self of each person is central to all persons. All otherness, all duality, all multiplicity is part of the play. Thus the lesson of this fantasy is that by a consistent thinking through of my fondest dreams for an explanation of this universe, and through an attempt to imagine as clearly as I can the nature of eternal bliss, I come right back to willing the place where I am! There is simply the proviso that all resentment for past and present suffering can be wiped out and turned into joy by waking up and finding that I, as the inmost Self, had deliberately dreamed it, and that it was an integral part of the delight which that Self enjoys through all eternity.

But, so long as I am just wishing and spinning a fantasy, I must consider this crucial question: do I want it arranged so that when I awaken to my true Self, the old ego is simply to evaporate? If I could awaken at some point before my death, the two identities would naturally run together. On the surface, I would remember my name, address, and telephone number, and recollect quite clearly that for "all practical purposes," that is, for carrying on a particular social game, I am still a limited individuality called Alan Watts. But concentric with this outward *persona*, this mask, I would be vividly aware that my basic identity—apprehended rather than comprehended—was the eternal Self of all selves.

And after death? Am I quite sure that I could be reconciled to the ultimate disappearance of this precious Alan Watts game in which I have invested so much time and energy? This is always a hard question for a *young* person, for he is not at that point in the rhythm of mortal time where he is ready to give up. He is set to continue as a matter of biological necessity, for the action of living requires "follow through" like the blow of the hand upon a drum: it aims beyond the skin. Willingness to vanish is incompatible with that spirit of "follow through," except in an individual who has vividly realized the eternal identity beneath the temporal. Furthermore, even an old man whose mind remains alert is always possessed by curiosity to know what will happen in the future, what new discoveries and creations the genius of man will bring forth, what course history will take, and what we shall find out about the inner secrets of the world.

Yet it seems to me that after several hundred years of this sort of thing, I might have altogether too much of that haven't-we-been-here-before feeling. Surely, those who insist on the supreme value of individual personality continuing forever have not fully thought through their desire. Such a wish is comparable to the increasing confusion of Manhattan—a city trying to grow by making its individual buildings higher and higher. But this reaches a point of diminishing returns, for, after a certain height, the gain in living space ceases, because more and more of the lower floor areas have to be taken up by elevators. In other words, the indefinite prolongation of the individual is bad design—architecturally, biologically, and psychologically. The entity that is supposed to be prolonged is not the individual but some greater organism in which he belongs, as our cells belong in our bodies. The tragedy of mortality lies in not being aware of this belonging, and, above all, in not having found one's true identity in the inmost Self. And if that is found, then the disappearance of the ego-mask beyond death is not, as it is sometimes called, *absorption* of the soul into the Godhead. Nothing is absorbed; there is simply clear recollection of That which one always is.

It is also obvious that the wish-fulfilling religion that I have invented is substantially identical with the central theme of Hindu mythology—the theme of Brahman, the supreme Self, manifesting itself cyclically as all these worlds. Furthermore, in the Hindu myth the stages through which the *maya* is developed correspond to the sort of progression that would be followed by the person who could dream whatever he wished. The cycle of time during which the worlds are manifested is, as we saw, the *kalpa,* lasting 4,320,000 years. The *kalpa* is divided into four *yugas,* named after the throws in the Indian game of dice: *krita* (the perfect throw of 4), *treta* (the throw of 3), *dvapara* (the throw of 2), and *kali* (the worst throw, of 1). The first epoch is thus the *krita yuga,* lasting 1,728,000 years, during which the *maya*-dream is a paradise of shadowless glory. The second epoch is the *treta yuga,* lasting 1,296,000 years, when, although the paradise remains, there emerge certain uncontrolled factors, surprises that are thus far pleasant, but contain the apprehension of something unwanted. The third epoch is the *dvapara yuga,* lasting 864,000 years, during which the negative principle of disorder attains equality with the principle of order. And in the fourth epoch, *kali yuga,* lasting 432,000 years, the principle of disorder is triumphant. At the end of this epoch the forces of destruction grow and grow in fury, until, at the very end, the universes are dissolved in fire. Whereupon the Brahman awakens from the *maya*-dream, and remains in luminous peace through another 4,320,000 years before beginning the cycle again.

Note, however, that the principle of disorder can claim only 1,296,000 years of the whole *kalpa:* a third of the *treta yuga,* a half of the *dvapara yuga,* and the whole of the *kali yuga,* amounting in all to one third of the *kalpa.* This is a chronological symbolism for the principle that the continuance of the game depends upon the subordination of disorder to order, so that the former may always be in the situation of being overcome by the latter, despite the dramatic moment in which it appears to have the victory, at the end of the *kali yuga.*[2]

The vivid experiences of the mystics may be our only means of testing the truth of religious and metaphysical hypotheses, but that is not an exploration to be carried out in a book. There is, perhaps, a significant bias in mystical writings toward the general view of the universe that I have suggested, and this would include such Christian mystics as John Scotus

[2] According to Heinrich Zimmer (6) the *kali yuga* began on Friday, February 18, 3102 B.C., which means that there are 426,935 more years of it to come! But be consoled—for as the *yugas* draw to their close, time passes faster and faster.

Erigena, St. Simeon Neotheologos, Eckhart, Nicolas Cusanus, Boehme, and perhaps even Teilhard de Chardin. But it is not the purpose of this essay to indulge in a metaphysical argument. I have nothing so earnest in mind as to insist that my point of view is the truth. The truth will out by its own self-evidence. My purpose is only to develop certain mythological constructions, such as the one I have just described, and then see what happens at the end. If, at that point, there is the conviction of some new insight into the universe and man, so much the better. Specifically, we are going to see what happens to a traditional and orthodox version of Christianity, to Catholicism,[3] if it is seen within the context of the scheme-of-things that I have been describing.

Whatever may be the rule in practice, is Christianity theoretically and dogmatically opposed to the idea that the creative activity of God is playful? Fortunately we can call at once to our aid the massive authority of St. Thomas Aquinas, writing about the Wisdom of God:

> The contemplation of wisdom is rightly compared with games for two things to be found in games. The first is that games give pleasure and the contemplation of wisdom gives the very greatest pleasure, according to what Wisdom says of itself in *Ecclesiasticus*, "My spirit is sweet above honey." The second is that the movements in games are not con-

---

[3] It is only fair to reveal my own prejudices, whereby the term "Catholicism" includes the Roman Catholic Church, the Eastern Orthodox Churches, and the Anglican Churches, because these are the principal Churches that center their worship around the altar as distinct from the pulpit. That is to say, they are still essentially "mystery religions," and not just societies for listening to lectures and promoting good works.

trived to serve another end, but are pursued for their own sake. It is the same with the delights of wisdom. . . . Hence divine Wisdom compares its delight to games, "I was with him forming all things and was delighted every day, playing before him at all times: playing in the world." (7)

The personified Wisdom of God who speaks in the books of *Ecclesiasticus* and *Proverbs* (whence St. Thomas' second quotation) is understood by the Church to be God the Son, the divine Logos "by whom all things were made."

Now, it is notorious that popular ideas of God's character are of a far lower moral standard than that by which we discern saintliness in men. The saint forgives "until seventy times seven" if anyone sins against him, but by many accounts the Lord does not forgive at all unless the offender grovels before him in an act of sincere contrition. The saint is above all urged not to take himself seriously, and, indeed, there is about all really holy people a kind of guileless humor, a sense of one's own absurdity which is not so much self-condemnation as pulling one's own leg. "The soul which is inwardly united to God," wrote St. Mark Podvizhnik, "becomes, in the greatness of its joy, like a good-natured simple-hearted child, and now condemns no one, Greek, heathen, Jew, nor sinner, but looks at them all alike with sight that has been cleansed, [and] finds joy in the whole world." (8) If, as Chesterton suggested, even the angels fly because they take themselves lightly, how much more must the Lord of the angels, the fountain of all virtues, be endowed with this particular virtue?

The ascription of a playful spirit to God may be

disconcerting to the devout because of the double meaning contained in the ideas of playing and not being serious. For on the one hand, this is a spirit of gaiety and exuberance, light-heartedness and joy. But on the other, the sense that something is *only* in play implies a certain shallowness, pretense, and even deceit. Similarly, not being serious may mean not being solemn, grave, pompous, or grim, but may also mean insincerity. Still another complication: deception is sometimes beneficent. The Sanskrit word *upaya* means cunning or deceit when used in a political context. But in the context of Hindu or Buddhist discipline it designates the "skillful means" which a teacher employs to help his students outwit their own egocentricity. In the same way, the biographies of the Christian saints abound in stories of overcoming the Devil by what St. Francis Xavier called "holy cunning." For in this case the Devil is one's own guile, one's own infinite capacity for looking at oneself looking at oneself looking at oneself, as when one is proud of being humble, proud of recognizing that one is proud of it, and proud of being subtle enough to see that the whole thing is an infinite regression.

Self-conscious tangles of this kind are, in all probability, mechanical defects in the nervous system, similar to the oscillations which occur in an electronic system when it tries to record itself in the act of recording. Thus when a television camera photographs its own receiver, the picture becomes a succession of "stuttering" waves, and the psychological or neurological equivalent would be the trembling, jittery state of anxiety, which is fearing fear or worrying about worry. This is the besetting problem of any reflexive or feed-back system—above all, of man's consciousness of himself—and the heart of the problem is that the process of self-consciousness cannot disentangle itself by itself. It has to be "tricked" out of its predicament. Private anxieties are instantly forgotten when a tornado strikes the neighborhood, but you cannot deliberately arrange a tornado, or its equivalent, to jolt yourself out of worries or pettinesses whenever they occur. You cannot surprise yourself on purpose, say, to get rid of hiccups. Someone or something beyond conscious control must overthrow the Devil at the right moment, for, being an archangel, he can read thoughts and is always aware of the intention that precedes the act. He can be defeated only by an act without prior intent. "Let not your left hand know what your right hand doeth."

Now in Christian terminology this "someone or something beyond conscious control" is called the grace of God, and grace is held to be the only means of overcoming the machinations of the Devil, that is, of the vicious circles into which self-consciousness can lead us. God as the giver of grace has therefore the same function as the *guru*, or spiritual guide, in Hinduism, and thus "the means of grace" would be the correct equivalent of *upaya*. But it does not seem to have occurred to most Christians that the means of grace might include trickery—that in his cure of souls the Lord might use placebos, jokes, shocks, deceptions, and all kinds of indirect and surprising methods of outwitting men's wonderfully defended egocentricity. (I am speaking now in purely Christian terms, on a level where we know nothing as yet of *tat tvam asi*.)

But, alas, the Lord is supposed to be totally devoid of wit or humor. His official utterances, the holy scriptures, are understood as if they were strictly Solemn Pronouncements—not, perhaps, to be taken quite literally, but certainly as bereft of any lightness of touch, innuendo, irony, exaggeration, self-caricature, leg-pulling, drollery, or merriment. Yet what if this show of solemnity is actually a sort of dead-pan expression? If the Lord is said to veil his glory, lest it be too bright for mortal eyes, might he not also veil his mirth—perhaps as something much, much too funny for men to stand?

> *"Al Padre, al Figlio, allo Spirito Santo"*
> *comincio "Gloria" tutto il Paradiso,*
> *si che m'inebbriava il dolce canto.*
> *Cio ch' io vedeva mi sembiava un riso*
> *dell' universo; per che mia ebbrezza*
> *entrava per l'udire e per lo viso.*[4]

If, then, as Dante suggests, the angels' hymn of praise to the Holy Trinity sounds like the laughter of the universe, what is the joke?

[4] "To Father, Son, and Holy Spirit," all Paradise began its song, "be glory!"—so that I was drunken with its sweetness. And what I saw before my eyes seemed a laughter of the universe; whereby my drunkenness found entrance through both sound and sight. *Paradiso*, xxvii, 1–6.

III

Who Is Responsible?

One day, when I was a very small boy, I was playing with sounds and discovered the delicious word "Blast." It was such a good word to linger over and to roll around the tongue. "Bull-lahst!" Then I went and played it to my mother. She went quite white, and I'll never forget the scary look in her eyes. "Don't *ever* say that!" she said. "It's against God." That was when I first discovered that words can be more powerful than deeds and more real than things.

"In the beginning was the Word." "And God *said*, Let there be light." "By the word of the Lord were the heavens made, and all the hosts of them by the breath of his mouth." "The grass withereth, the flower fadeth; but the word of our God shall stand for ever."

For Logos, the Word, is God the Son, the Second Person of the Trinity, the archetypal design and pattern of the universe, the Law of the Lord, the creative Agent "by whom all things were made."

It is thus that, in the whole tradition of Hebrew and Christian ideas, the supernatural world is related to the natural in somewhat the same way that words are related to things and events. Ordinarily, one would suppose that things and events came first, and that words were later invented to describe them, to stand for them—like money for wealth. But in the philosophy of the Bible, it is just the reverse. The word comes first, for it is the name of the thing, which, when uttered by God, brings the thing into being. It is an outcome of this tradition that, in the West, we have long thought of natural events as expressions of law, that, putting it rather naïvely, nothing happens except in obedience to a commandment, and that therefore the laws of nature are laid down in advance of all happenings, to be the foundation of the world, or the tracks upon which events should run.

This is not, of course, the thinking of the most modern West, of scientists in the twentieth century. For today we speak of the laws of nature quite figuratively—not as ordinances which events obey, but as human ways of describing and measuring regularities in the behavior of the physical world. We find it redundant to attribute this regularity to anything beyond the events concerned; nothing *makes* them regular; they simply *are* regular, in the same way that quadrupeds regularly have four legs, or otherwise would not be called quadrupeds. To discern regularities in the physical world is the easiest way to make sense of it, and to know where you are. If you count a hundred paces between your home and the river, and assume that the two will stay put, you can find your home in the dark. But the paces came *after* the house, the river, and the land between.

Yet, because measurements and descriptions of the physical world give one apparent control of the world, it is natural to suppose that their power may be greater than the powers of nature, and that nature is an expression of the word-power of a Supreme Intelligence which is, in itself, a kind of verbal organism. Ordinarily, one would say that the meaning of a word is something nonverbal, some physical thing or event. But, from another point of view, it is precisely words that give meaning to the world. Language in its broadest sense, including words, numbers, signs, and symbols of all kinds, is what peculiarly distinguishes men from animals, and enables us to know that we know. Language is the symbolic echo of direct experience, lending to it a resonance that enhances it—as a great cathedral, with its subtle reverberations, lends an other-worldly magnificence to the voice of a choir.

From the standpoint of the Christian West, symbols are the supremely civilizing agency: I may love you with all my heart, but my love is as dumb as a brute's until words give it expression. Thus, a person is cultured to the extent that he looks at people and buildings and landscapes with the words of poets and philosophers in the back of his mind. For they enable him to see the world in a new and particular way, just as painters, with their visual symbolisms, have taught us to see that certain natural scenes look "just like a picture!" Nature is, according to this view, beloved to the extent that she reminds us of the works of artists. I am that much poorer if, when I look at the stars, there is not somewhere echoing in the back of my brain:

> O look at all the fire-folk, sitting in the air!
> The bright boroughs, the circle-citadels there!

In the Western world, all that is spiritual is associated with symbols—with words, ideas, concepts, designs and abstractions. The physical universe is an incarnation of the Word, a gross replica of ideas in the mind of God—a process of bright, pure, and lucid form trying to express itself in the medium of intractable sludge and rubble. The supernatural domain is a sphere of transparent clarity and intelligibility, of pure ideation, an articulation of light and form so exquisite that the music of Bach and the intellectual architecture of St. Thomas are, as the latter said, by comparison straw. Furthermore this supernatural sphere has an infinitely higher degree of reality and permanence than the physical sphere. To earthbound senses it may seem to be diaphanous and vague, but beside it the stars themselves are no more than falling sparks.

This will explain the peculiar fact that the religious exercises of Jews and Christians are so largely verbal. Hindus and Buddhists will chant a little, and then enter into silent meditation so as to change the level and quality of consciousness. But Jewish and Christian services are almost entirely streams of utterance —praying, singing, reading, and preaching. Should silence occur, except in a Quaker meeting, it usually denotes some hitch in the arrangements, and the organist keeps things alive by "inkling," that is, by an unostentatious improvisation on the theme of a chant or hymn. Even private prayers are, for the most part, spoken formulae. But because, at least in traditional forms of worship, the prayers are based upon the words of the holy scriptures, the Christian philosophy of prayer is that it is the Holy Spirit which speaks through the mouth of the worshiper. For worship is the process of man's being gathered up into the eternal dialogue of love between the Persons of the Trinity.

The supremacy of the Word is especially evident in the differing modes of transmission for temporal power and for spiritual power. The king transmits his power to his son, through right of birth, but, as is well known, the good qualities of the father do not necessarily pass by heredity to the son. The biological process cannot, it is felt, be trusted, and therefore wisdom and law must be passed on and maintained by some more reliable form of succession. Thus temporal power is overshadowed by spiritual power, where the succession is determined, not by birth, but by study and examinations culminating in ordination. Furthermore, it is often the rule that the priest identifies himself completely with his role, taking the side of the Word instead of the flesh so thoroughly that he becomes a celibate, and has no natural issue.

The ideal of this philosophy of the Word is the transfiguration of the body and of the whole physical universe. It is to make the material world more and more conformable to the supernatural world—that is to say, obedient to the Word of God. It is to put reason over instinct, intellect over passion, and grace over nature—not so that instinct, passion, and nature are annihilated, but so that they become servants of the Word, like well-trained horses. Western technology is, in its basic motivation, the direct outcome of this philosophy. It is first of all the aim of science to translate (transfigure?) all natural processes into words or mathematical formulae, thereby making the whole world intelligible. Once this has been done, the irregularities and rough edges of the world can be conformed to an ideal pattern of how things *should* be. This is the work of technology, a wonder-working in the direct line of descent from the miracles of Jesus and the saints. Christianity is, after all, the only religion that takes its miracles seriously.

The philosophy of the Word also lies behind technology in the sense that it looks at the universe in terms of models taken from the arts and crafts. For God is seen as the architect, the potter, the carpenter, and the smith. The Bible abounds in such images. "Woe unto him that striveth with his Maker! . . . Shall the clay say to him that fashioneth it, What makest thou?" "Behold, the Lord stood upon a wall made by a plumbline, with a plumbline in his hand." "When he prepared the heavens, I was there: when he set a compass upon the face of the depth."

Where wast thou when I laid the foundations of the earth?
    declare, if thou hast understanding.
Who hath laid the measures thereof, if thou knowest?
    or who hath stretched the line upon it?
Whereupon are the foundations thereof fastened?
    or who laid the corner stone thereof? (*Job* 38:4–6. AV.)

"For he is like a refiner's fire, . . . and he shall sit as
a refiner and purifier of silver: and he shall purify the
sons of Levi."

> My substance was not hid from thee, when I was
> made in secret, and curiously wrought in the low-
> est parts of the earth.
> Thine eyes did see my substance, yet being un-
> perfect; and in thy book all my members were
> written. (*Psalm* 139: 15–16. AV.)

Accordingly, the design, the Logos, was there in the
mind of the Maker, even before the work was begun,
and the material creation is therefore a construct,
manufactured according to plan. *Deus faber.*

This entire cosmology seems to represent a particular development of human consciousness that must
have taken place during two or three thousand years,
or more. It represents the transition from living by
instinct and impulse to the attempt to live by thought
and reflection. It represents man's growing realization
of the power of language and symbols, and, in particular, the stage of this growth where the power of the
word is utterly fascinating. It represents the emergence of a strong sense of the individual ego, and of
its capacity to change and control external events and
internal passions by efforts of will. It represents,
above all, the birth of that special type of human consciousness which we associate with Western civilization—a consciousness that is, on the one hand, analytical and sharply focused, and, on the other, very
much turned back upon itself: a consciousness that is
embarrassingly self-conscious.

There are two principal ways in which the power
of the Word assists this type of consciousness. The

first is that words provide a notation for a style of consciousness based on noticing. The foundation of analytical thinking is *attention;* to attend, to notice, is to focus consciousness sharply upon some restricted area. It is to use the mind like a spotlight, illuminating the world bit by bit—keeping the bits organized and classified by the system of tags or pigeonholes which words provide. The second is that words give us a model or symbol of the world which is much easier to understand than the world itself. It is much less wiggly and capricious. It reduces experience to a comprehensible form in somewhat the same way that carving meat with a knife makes it more edible. Despite Korzybski's insistence that $Fido_1$ must be clearly distinguished from $Fido_2$, how necessary it is to be able to classify Fido as Dog. The verbal description of the world is a simplified, albeit oversimplified, model of the world. But it provides us with a platform apart from the world itself, upon which we can stand and take a new look at the world. Words representing things make it possible to have thoughts about experiences, to deal with life in terms of symbols as we deal with wealth in terms of money.

The initial advantages of this mode of consciousness are sensational, for it is the foundation of all craft and culture. It enables us to make order out of the confused spray of the stars, and to predict the seasons and the changes of weather. Words and symbols are magical savers of time and effort otherwise spent in pointing at things, drawing them, or dragging them around in the intellectual equivalent of barter. It is no wonder at all that words have been felt to be supernatural, and, because of their astonishing power, to have greater reality and antiquity than the material universe. But this, possibly superstitious, conception has had quite remarkable consequences for the further development of consciousness. It has laid the foundations for anxiety and guilt. It has made it possible for man to compare himself as he is with himself as he should be, and to realize that the world of events falls far, far short of the rationality, simplicity, orderliness and intelligibility of the world of words.

Thousands of years ago, the demonstrable efficiency of rational thought and of the rule of law in social conduct must have cast doubt upon the impulses and intuitions of man's organic and non-reflective being. On the one hand, there arose the anxiety of choosing between hunch and the reasoned course. The choice would have been relatively simple were hunch always a natural self-interest, and the reasoned course always the interest of society. But, on the other hand, there was always the nagging suspicion that the reasoned course might not be reasoned enough, that important factors might have been left out of consideration, or that there might have been a false step in calculation. Add to this the intimation that hunch deals with some situations much better than reason, especially the situations which are so complicated and fast-moving that words cannot keep track of them. In the moment that man doubts his immediate impulse, there is no end to complexities. For what else will he trust? Intelligence? But by what does one test one's intelligence? Information? But how does one know that one has enough information? Inspiration? But how does one know whether it is of

God or of the Devil? Worse still, from that first moment of doubt there is no going back. Innocence is then and there lost, and all possibility of return is prevented by the angel with the flaming sword. Beyond this point, the only strength is to be able to contain and endure anxiety.

And then there is guilt. The unavoidable drip, drip, drip of the certainty that something quite undefined has gone wrong, and that *you* did it. Somewhere, far off in a half-remembered past that may be only a fantasy, was the time when the immediate impulse was inspired wisdom. Even if it led to instant death, that death was splendid. The radiant defeat of vegetation at autumn. Glory of fire that destroys the moth. Succeeding or failing by the merely chronological and quantitative criterion of survival was of no import at all. For the man living by pure impulse was perfect in every motion—like the foam patterns of breaking waves, the markings upon shells, and the walk of cats. But he didn't know it.

To know, and to know that you know, means paying attention; it means concentrating on the motions of life one step, one wiggle, one pulse at a time so as to figure them out. But just as soon as this narrowed and bright attention has figured out *how* it is that we live and move, think and speak, the process no longer happens of itself. From then on, we are responsible. We must *make* it happen, and decide through the pain of thought what course it shall take. From then on we move with constant anxiety, because we never know for sure what is right, and with constant guilt, because we are nonetheless responsible, and because in the instant that we become responsible something goes deeply and strangely wrong.

We began to play God—that is, to control our lives instead of letting them happen. And God said, "Very well, then, take over. You're on your own." But we were like the Sorcerer's Apprentice, and didn't really know what to do. Thereupon pain ceased to be ecstasy and became punishment. At the same time, we began to feel responsible for dying. Death was no longer the transformation and renewal of life, the shuffling of the pack for a new deal. Death became the mark of *failure*, the wages of sin, and the result of our incompetence in playing God.

Yet the secret behind the scenes, which the flaming sword of guilt prevents us from finding out, is that this is actually God playing man. The narrowing of attention was omniscience (in the Hindu sense) contracting into ego, there to become fascinated—as the hypnotist fascinates by holding the mind to one point —spellbound, enchanted, and paralyzed. God entranced himself and forgot the way back, so that now he feels himself to be man, playing—guiltily—at being God. For to attend is also to ignore and to forget: it is to notice the figure, and to ignore its inseparable background; to see the inside so clearly that one forgets its outside; to feel oneself in the body alone, and no longer in the cosmos that goes with it. My better half appears to be a universe into which I have been cast as a stranger. I no longer understand it intuitively, and am compelled to make sense of it bit by bit. In this predicament, the Word is my salvation. Having forgotten how to live, I need to know the rules. Having forgotten how to dance, I need a diagram of the steps. I don't even know how to make love any more, and my parents are embarrassed when telling me.

It is thus that man's wisdom is not handed down from generation to generation by heredity, but by the recorded word, which reposes in a supernatural domain outside the spontaneous impulses of the body. Such is the facility of words that this wisdom is, in one highly specialized direction, far more complex and effective than the hereditary skills of animals. It enables man to change his environment and his own behavior on a scale without precedent in nature. But once he has started, he is compelled to go on. It is not only that man *can* change the world; the problem is that he *must*, and that he does not really know how to do it. For the Word is deceptive. It tells what, but not how. And the Law, the book of rules, is even worse. It tells you that you must deliberately do certain things, such as loving, which are only satisfactory when they happen spontaneously. Therefore you must see to it that they happen spontaneously. "Thou *shalt* love the Lord thy God"—not just ritually, but "with all thy heart, and with all thy soul, and with all thy might."

The predicament is admirably described in St. Paul's *Epistle to the Romans,* from which the following crucial passage is freely translated from the saint's abominable Greek:

> What, then, shall we say? Is the Law sin? Indeed, no! But I would never have known sin except *through* the Law; for I would not have recognized lust unless the Law had said, "You shall not lust."

But sin made this precept an occasion to bring out in me every kind of lust, for without the Law sin was dead [i.e., unconscious]. Once [in my innocence] I was alive without the Law; but with the coming of the precept sin revived, and I died, and discovered that the precept of life brought death. For sin, by means of the precept, deceived and slew me. Yet for this very reason the Law is holy, and the precept is holy, and just and good.

Was, then, this good thing [the cause of] my dying? Indeed, no! But sin worked death in me through the good [precept] that it might be shown to *be* sin; that sin, by means of the precept, might become [known to be] exceedingly sinful. For we know that the Law is spiritual—but I am of the flesh, sold out to sin. For I do not intend the things that I do. What I will, I do not, but what I hate, I do. If, then, I do *not* do what I will [to do], I am [at least] recognizing the excellence of the Law; and then it is no longer I that act, but sin dwelling in me. For I know that nothing good dwells in me —that is, in my flesh. I can readily will, but I cannot *produce* goodness. The good that I would, I do not; but the evil that I would not, I do. So, if I do what I would not, it is no more *I* that do it, but sin dwelling in me.

Therefore I discover the principle that in my willing to do the good, the evil is with me. For I delight in the Law of God in my inmost being; but I see another law in my members, warring against the law of my mind, and making me the captive of that sinful law in my members. Wretched man that I am! Who will rescue me from this body of death? (*Romans* 7: 7–24.)

Now, if this predicament is not simply an insane vicious circle, what is it? It is obviously an adventure in the growth of consciousness, and, above all, of self-knowledge. The Lord becomes entranced in his own *maya,* but, because he *is* the Lord, he can never be captured ultimately. For in the most expert and subtle way he makes his bondage and the means of release one and the same. He projects his own God-head outwardly, to be something wholly above and beyond himself. In this way he undergoes the adventure of being lost, flung far out from his own center, and involved in the toils of the most fascinating of all insoluble puzzles: to control life, to will love, to know *how.* At the same time, the God that he projects into the supernatural world above acts as his *guru* and Savior. But the supreme method, the royal road of all *gurus* and spiritual masters, is to make the fool become wise by persisting most consistently in his folly, until it reaches a complete *reductio ad absurdum.* This projected God, who is the Lord of the Bible and the supreme object of Christian and Jewish worship, is also the skillful *guru* and master of "holy cunning."

All this is quite clear in the marvelous tale of the creation, and of the fall of Adam. Note that, at this point, the Lord is not working according to a preconceived plan. The creation is perfectly spontaneous. Every stage of it surprises him. Only when it is done does he see that it is good. "And God created great whales (oops!), and every living creature that moveth, which the waters brought forth abundantly, after their kind, and every winged fowl after his kind: and God saw that it was good." When the Lord has his whole *maya* arranged before him, including the clay figurine of Adam, made in his own image, he comes and breathes *himself* into Adam's nostrils, for the "breath of life" is the *ruach Adonai,* the same Spirit

of God which, in the beginning, moved upon the face
of the waters. Thereupon the Lord looks out of the
eyes of the figurine; but he has forgotten who he is,
and therefore sees himself walking in the garden just
as if he were someone else. The Lord is now entranced, and his *alter ego*, the bearded Old Gentleman in the long robe, initiates the long, long process
of his awakening, which is, at the same time, his
bondage.

There really was no need to mention the Tree of
Knowledge. It would have been a safe risk that Adam
would never have noticed it if the Lord hadn't
brought the subject up. But when the Lord not only
called attention to it, but also issued terrifying warn-
ings about the consequences of eating its fruit, it became perfectly certain that Adam would try it.

Something of this kind happens over and over
again in fairy tales. The hero invariably transgresses
the Terrible Prohibition—not to look behind, not to
open the golden box, not to take the short cut through
the wood—for otherwise there would be no story.
The Lord, in his wisdom, knew quite enough about
human nature to know exactly what he was doing,
and that all perfectly unreasonable prohibitions are
invitations to adventure. It would have been quite a
different matter if he had commanded Adam not to
pull Eve's hair, or not to eat their own children.

Instead, the Lord fixed upon a particular tree
which, after all, he himself had planted, and forbade
Adam to eat its fruit lest he attain the knowledge of
good and evil, and with it the curse of death. Now,
the words for "good" and "evil" in the original Hebrew have a special connection with craftsmanship

and skill; they denote what is advantageous or disadvantageous, skillful or clumsy, cunning or crude, from a technical point of view. Those who ate the fruit would become "as gods," for they would know how to control events and how to make things happen. This is why Adam's fall and expulsion from the garden involves the curse of work, for once you start controlling things according to your deliberations, you can no longer rely upon impulse. You must stop playing, and be serious. You must think of the future, and plan for it, and thus become aware of death in an altogether new way—as a dragon lying at the end of the passage, as the final humiliation of all that *you*, by your skill, have achieved and controlled. Life becomes the putting-off of death; and so begins the reign of anxiety.

How clear this becomes when Jesus advocates a way of life which is the precise opposite, though his startling doctrine loses much of its force in the familiar translation. More literally, if less sonorously, he says:

> This is why I'm telling you: don't worry about your life, what you're going to eat or what you're going to drink, or about your body, what you're going to wear. Isn't life more than food, and the body than clothes?
>
> Look at the wild birds: they don't sow, they don't reap, they don't harvest in barns, and yet your Father in heaven feeds them. Aren't you much more important than they? Which of you, by worrying, can add one span to his lifetime?
>
> And why do you worry about clothes? Learn from the meadow lilies, how they flourish: they don't work, they don't spin, and yet I'm telling you that even Solomon in all his splendor wasn't robed like

any one of them. Now if this is how God clothes the wild grass, which lives today and is thrown into the oven tomorrow, how much better [will he look after] you, faithless ones?

So don't worry, saying "What are we going to eat?" or "What are we going to drink?" or "What are we going to wear?" for these are all the things that the crowd goes for, though your Father in heaven knows that you need them. First seek for the kingdom and for his justice, and you will get all those things anyhow. And don't worry about tomorrow, for tomorrow will take care of itself; let trouble wait for its own day. (*Matthew* 6: 25–34.)

That is quite one of the most subversive passages in the Bible, and no "sensible" person would dream of following it, for it stands in complete opposition to the life of work, control, plans, provisions, and savings. But the real challenge of this passage is that when the gospel of the nonserious life is put in the form of a commandment, we are forced to discover exactly why it is that we cannot obey, and at just what point we put up the blocks against letting go. Once the fruit has been eaten, and once the life of impulse has been called in question, there is no going back. There is only going on, by the way of fuller and fuller consciousness.

But the way of consciousness is the way of effort, and, as is all too well known, men will seldom, if ever, make a supreme effort for some positive good; they will make it only to avoid some desperate evil. Taxes for guns are far more easily levied than taxes for cakes and ale all round. It is therefore essential that there be an Enemy, charged with fulfilling a most complex role, a role of many-aspected ambivalence, which is at once suggested in the fact that the name of our enemy, the Devil, is Lucifer, the Bringer of Light. (In Greek, Phosphorus, which also means the Morning Star.)

Before we go any further, it must be clearly understood that from the standpoint of *official* Christianity no good word can be said for the Devil. Officially, the Devil has no *necessary* part to play in the fulfillment of God's purposes; the Devil bears full responsibility for bringing evil into the universe, and although God permitted this to happen, in no sense whatever did he start it or condone it; the Devil was originally a bright angel who fell from heaven because of pride and maliciousness cooked up entirely by his own will and out of his own mind. This is exactly what the official position should be, because it is the position of taking the drama seriously. For when we forget the proscenium arch, or at least put it far into the backs of our minds, we feel that the actor playing the villain is truly villainous. This illusion is the whole point of the play.

Yet, since we are pursuing a metatheology, we must go off stage into the green room and see what happens before the play begins, and after it ends. I have suggested that the fundamental dynamics of the universe is the game of hide-and-seek, lost-and-found, or peek-a-boo, the play of yes-and-no, positive-and-negative, up-and-down, which goes on and on because the light side overcomes the dark side again and again, and is light only so long as it does so. Explicitly (that is, on stage), the light and the dark are enemies, but implicitly (off stage), they are not only friends, not only twins, not only co-conspirators, but constitute a unity which cannot be described, since every word, every label, designates what is *in* some class. There is no word that designates the inside and the outside of a class simultaneously, in such a way as to describe the complete inseparability of the two. But, if I may be so bold as to say so, the final metaphysical secret is that the boundary between all insides and all outsides is held in common by both—that insides are not found without outsides, nor outsides without insides. This invariable inseparability of things quite different from each other seems to imply some sort of hidden conspiracy, some agreement, some unity of essence behind the scenes.

Tweedledum and Tweedledee *agreed* to have a battle.

On the other hand, the *game* of hide-and-seek—the art of drama—consists in making believe, either that the light side can obliterate the dark (and they lived happily ever after), or that there is a real danger of the dark side obliterating the light (but deliver us from evil). Therefore, when the Lord God and the Devil come out officially—that is, in their ceremonial or dramatic roles—they are implacable foes; but may we not, as a *hintergedanke* (as a suspicion far, far in the backs of our minds), suppose that in the green room of heaven, before the show of creation began, there was an Original Agreement?

There was God the Father, with God the Son sitting at his right hand. No one ever mentions who sits at his left hand; but of course it was Lucifer, Satan, Samma-el, who, in the older books of the Bible, is simply the agent of the Lord's wrath, his left, sinister, and inauspicious hand that does all the necessary dirty work. So we may suppose, then, that God the Father instructed both of them in their roles, explaining how he himself would have to appear to take the side of his Son—for this is, of course, what ensures that light will continually outshine darkness, even though it cannot shine without darkness. He told them that, on this particular round of the Creation, they were to stir up a drama that would have the audience screaming in its seats (and we know, don't we, who is the audience?), so that when at last the curtain fell all would swear that this was the best show they had ever seen.

Would not, therefore, the Lord arrange that the Left Hand Man appear in an unusually loathsome guise, first of all in the form of a serpent, and later as a black, bat-winged goat-man? In the beginning he is to appear as the implacable Enemy of the Lord and of his Creation—the Tempter, the Author of Evil, and the Father of Lies. Later, he is to appear also as the Chief Executioner and Torturer of all the demons and souls he has beguiled. He is to think up the most repulsive and obscene punishments, under which his followers will supposedly shriek in unimaginable agony forever. So, the Director would allow the Villain (as Prince of *this* World) to steal the show, putting the audience in peril of everlasting damnation, and to play so convincingly that the proscenium arch would be clean forgotten.

If, then, we keep the idea of the Original Agreement in the backs of our minds, the various stories about the origin of evil become curiously suggestive —principally because of their odd vagueness as to what the original evil actually was. Most theologians agree that Lucifer's sin was pride, and, specifically, pride in its most noxious form—spiritual pride. By some accounts, the actual occasion of his fall was his objection to the "contamination" of spirit with flesh in the creation of mankind. It is said that he rebelled against an act of God which seemed to him an indignity to spirit. He was therefore expelled from heaven, and became the arch-enemy of the human race. An Islamic version has it that Lucifer loved God more than did all the other angels together, and, for this reason, could not bear the prospect that the divine spirit should dwell in the hairy, animal bodies of men. He was therefore cast into hell, and the only thing that sustains him in torment is his memory of the expression of God's eye and the sound of God's voice as he uttered the dread sentence, "Begone!"

Spiritual pride and disobedience are likewise held to be the occasion of Adam's fall—spiritual pride in that he aspired to become as a god "knowing both good and evil," and disobedience in that he was warned not to eat from the Tree. Theologians seldom favor the popular notion that original sin was the awakening of sexual desire: that the serpent was the phallus, the fruit sexual pleasure, and shame in nakedness the subsequent sense of guilt. The Bible says that Adam "knew" his wife, Eve, only after expulsion from the garden, but this popular interpretation of the story has much to be said for it. The real trouble with all these theories is that they make the primal sin impossibly tame. Lucifer was perhaps, like Shiva in some of the Puranic tales, the arch-ascetic who could not go along with the Lord's love for his *maya*, with the sensuality of a marriage between Heaven (the male) and Earth (the female), for, as we have been told, "God so loved the world." Lucifer would then be the force against creation, the agent of death to all that is not pure spirit.

But the more subtle theologians warn us that the Devil is, after all, an angel of the highest degree, one who has looked into the very heart of the Divine Being, and is therefore versed in mysteries of which we know nothing. Just, then, as the glory of God is beyond all description and comprehension, so, conversely, there is a "mystery of iniquity" which is comparably ineffable and beyond human imagination. Terms like "spiritual pride" and "malice" refer, when applied to the Devil, to atrocities and depravities so abysmally evil that we would neither recognize them if we saw them, nor understand them if they were explained. The nearest we can ever get to this order of things is perhaps in certain psychotic states where everything appears to be indescribably *strange*—shapes, emotions, attitudes, rhythms and gestures so downright odd that they bear not the least resemblance to the familiar world of sane consciousness. Think of a peculiar taste—not sweet, not sour, not bitter, not stinky like limburger, but just horribly unclassifiable—a taste that clings and cloys and won't be done away with. This, say the very subtle theologians, is the sort of menace we are dealing with in the person of the Devil, and the more we cease to pry into it, and instead cling firmly to the grace of God, the better.

The *grimoires* and arcane books of demonology suggest that the true preoccupation of diabolism is not just destroying, but insulting and humiliating the created order of things by upsetting the laws of nature. Thus the Witches' Sabbath was supposed to be an orgy in which the initiates of an infernal mystery acquired power to transform their bodies into shapes that were half dog, half bat, half fish, half worm, or half spider, and, in general, to turn human flesh into a kind of ooze that responds to every perverse whim of the will. But note that the nearer we come to describing the supposedly ineffable mysteries of evil, all turns into comedy. These "infernal orgies" turn out to be no different in principle from a group of children laughing themselves silly over the game of who can make the most horrible face.

No, the whole point of the ineffability of the Devil's real intentions and of his primordial sin is that the sense of guilt is the most disquieting to an accused person when the nature of his crime is unstated. . . . "We will not go into the details of the charge against you. . . . After all, this is a public courtroom, and there are just some things that cannot be mentioned, because their obscenity and depravity is an outrage, not only to the most elementary decency, but to the very order of nature. . . . You, the accused, deny it as you may, know very well what you have done, and the circumstances of your unmentionable crime give every evidence of its having been coldly intended and deliberately planned—planned, furthermore, in the fullest knowledge that what you did was in clear opposition to the laws of both God and man. . . ." [1]

---

[1] Strange to say, there are still states in which a man can be sent to prison for a misdeed no more specifically defined than "that infamous crime against nature, committed by man with man." Presumably this should cover a bad haircut, or partnership in a factory that pollutes a river.

Clearly, the whole force of original, existential guilt is that it be an obscure and gnawing sense of being profoundly in the wrong, though for no discernible reason. Governments maintain this sense in a mild form by seeing to it that the laws are so complex that every citizen is inadvertently guilty of some crime, making it possible to convict anyone when convenient. Religions do it much more thoroughly, often suggesting that one's very existence is in some way an effrontery and an offense against God. "O God, forasmuch as without thee we are unable to please thee. . . ." "If we say that we have no sin, we deceive ourselves, and the truth is not in us." "Enter not into judgment with thy servant, O Lord, for in thy sight shall no man living be justified." "Behold, I was shapen in wickedness: and in sin hath my mother conceived me."

It makes no difference that being born in sin was the fault, not of God, but of Lucifer or Adam in some remote age; the actual effect of the idea of Original Sin is to feel that natural existence is in some way both a fault and one's own fault.

But, of course, the something awful that has gone wrong and which must not be mentioned is, in reality (that is, in God), the production of the original illusion in which the Creator seems to become the creature, the act of hiding in the game of hide-and-seek. The same act is, on other levels, the narrowing of attention to engender the conscious ego, and the loss of faith in spontaneous impulse. Yet, what is more, the apprehension of this act of hiding as a nameless evil for which we feel deeply guilty, is in fact a way of ensuring that the game shall not end too soon. It confirms us in the sense of separate individuality and responsibility. It is the flaming sword that turns in all directions and guards the way of return to Paradise, preventing us from daring to recognize, upon pain of the utmost blasphemy, that we are each the Lord in hiding. Before we can have the courage to attain that recognition, we must follow the difficult way of consciousness and the discipline of the Word to the point where the ego's pride in itself is entirely debunked, not masochistically, but in the spirit of cosmic humor. Without this particular deflation of the ego, we might imagine ourselves to be one with a God who takes himself seriously.

IV

How *Must* We Have Faith?

Before going further, I have to explain some of the rudimentary principles of Christianity—specifically, something called the Incarnation, which is offered as the solution to man's "fallen" state. I hope this will not be tedious. But, during several years' experience as a university chaplain, I discovered that the educated bourgeoisie of the Western world is religiously illiterate. This includes many theological students, not only when they begin their studies, but also when they finish.

While it is true that some of the basic attitudes of Judaism and Christianity have sunk deeply into the common sense of most Western people, it cannot be assumed that even regular church-goers have so much as an elementary grasp of the doctrines they profess. The reason is mainly that the language, form and style of these ideas have become so foreign to our ways of thinking that they are meaningless even to very intelligent people.

To begin at the beginning of the trouble, it is utterly incomprehensible that one man's disobedience should have involved the entire race in the guilt for his sin, and, what is more, made them liable to the penalty of everlasting damnation. This seems in flat opposition to all our ideas of personal responsibility and integrity, the more so when there is no explanation of the channels whereby the taint of original sin passes from generation to generation. It is even more impossible to discover any connection between one's personal salvation from hell and the firm belief that a certain Jesus of Nazareth was born of a virgin. Two things could hardly be more unrelated. I am not trying to dispute the validity of these doctrines—only to say that to most educated moderns they are perfectly weird.

More astonishing still than the transmission of original sin is the notion that we are in some way saved by the death of Jesus Christ upon the cross. How is this rather remote historical event connected with our personal problems? How was death a sacrifice and a torment to a person who was supposed to be the Son of God and a worker of fabulous miracles? How is this sacrifice connected with God's love for each one of us personally? In what way does it tie in with our taking part in a ceremony where— somewhat cannibalistically—we eat his body and drink his blood in the form of bread and wine? And why can't we reap the mysterious benefits of these extraordinary events without undergoing the formality of having water poured on us with an incantation? Is all this just so much highly improbable miraculous behavior, which God asks us to believe as a test of our faith? If so, why didn't he make it *really* improbable, such as having to believe that the far side of the moon is covered with an enormous umbrella?

Note that the difficulties arise in seeing the connections, the relationships between these ideas. For they represent methods of thinking or forms of logic based on symbolic correspondences which we no longer use in our reasoning. When I used to examine candidates for the ministry, I sometimes asked such questions as, "What is the relationship between the Virgin Birth, the Resurrection, and the Holy Communion?" I used to get such answers as that the Holy Communion service *mentioned* the other two events! Only rarely did theological graduates have some idea of the way in which these doctrines are tied together; their education gave them no grasp of the basic rationale or design of their religion. It was all bits and pieces.

Christianity therefore impresses the modern Westerner as the most impossibly complicated amalgamation of odd ideas, and though it is his spiritual birthright and the faith of his fathers, it is very much easier to help him understand Buddhism or Vedanta, which I have taught—and, I imagine, Islam or Judaism. Furthermore, he is apt to find something indefinably embarrassing about the emotional atmosphere generated around clergymen and churches. How can one quite put a finger on it? Is it moralistic sentimentality—something unctuous, something sanctimonious, something clothesy, undancing, straitlaced, and against the loveliness of the human body? Whatever it may be, it is the plainly identifiable stink of piety.

Still more important, it is quite obvious to the canny observer that most Christians, including clergy and devout laity, do not believe in Christianity. If they did, they would be screaming in the streets, taking daily full-page advertisements in the newspapers, and subscribing for the most hair-raising television programs every night of the week. Even Jehovah's Witnesses are polite and genteel in their door-to-door propaganda. Nobody, save perhaps a few obscure fanatics, is *really* bothered by the idea that every man is constantly haunted by an angelic fiend, more imminently dangerous and malicious than the most depraved agents of the Nazis. Most people are sinners and unbelievers, and will probably go to hell. So what? Let God worry about that one!

Today the Western world is post-Christian. The Churches are huge, prosperous organizations, and, aside from expanding their memberships and building new plants, their chief concern is the preservation of family ties and sexual mores. Their influence on major problems of domestic and international politics is minimal. Outside Quaker meetings and Catholic monasteries, there is hardly the slightest concern for the inner life, for the raising of human consciousness to union with God—supposedly the main work of religion. Their politicking and lobbying is largely preoccupied with the maintenance of idiotic sumptuary laws against gambling, drinking, whoring, selling contraceptives, procuring abortions, dancing on Sundays, getting divorced or practicing homosexuality. True, there is some interest in Pealism ("get fat through faith") and in the *gemütlich* atmosphere of hymn-sings and revivals. But all this is irrelevant to the peculiar predicament of mankind in this century. Or any century.

If this sounds like a prophetic tirade, it is not meant to be. Everyone is at liberty to enjoy being irrelevant, to make sexuality the plum in involved competitive games, to goose themselves with the fear of the dreadful temptations of the flesh, and to wallow in being lovingly chastised by our Heavenly Father. My point is only that if Christians want to stick to these irrelevancies, the Church will shortly become a museum, and an exotic game of being the innest ingroup. Would it be merely sentimental to regret this? It is not simply that I do not want Canterbury, Chartres, Vézelay, and San Marco to become museums, like Santa Sophia in Constantinople and Sainte-Chappelle in Paris. My regret is rather that we shall never see the rich potentialities of this way of life fulfilled, nor realize that the Christian mythos has the possibility of blossoming into the most joyously exuberant, swinging, colorful, and liberated religion there ever was. Heaven need not wait for the grave.

But to reach the point of even seeing such a possibility, the basic design of traditional Christianity must first become clear; only in terms of this design can the particular dogmas, doctrines and symbols be related together. I would like, then, to begin by trying to straighten out the symbolism of the First Adam and the Second Adam, of the Fall of Man and its relation to the central Christian idea of the Incarnation.

However one interprets the story of the Fall of Man, literally or figuratively, or whether one feels that its immediate cause was a deed of willful malice or the forgetting of man's divine nature—the theologians are almost unanimous in feeling that it flung humanity into a vicious circle. Let me repeat the essential characteristics of this predicament.

The Fall was the acquisition of technique and self-awareness. It led men to mistrust their immediate impulses and to try to rely on conscious rationality. But they could not fully trust rationality, for they knew it was based upon deeper and still unknown reaches of the mind. They knew, too, that rationality could most easily become rationalization. To mistrust oneself leads, in due course, to mistrusting mistrust, and thus to being very mixed up indeed.

It led to the "curse of work." That is to say, once a process of deliberate interference with the natural environment has been started, it cannot be stopped. Technology leads to the necessity for more and more technology, for it is a battle with the Hydra monster: for every head chopped off, seven new ones appear.

It led to the infinite regressions of moral duplicity, generated by the oscillating echo phenomena of a self-awareness that, being combined with self-mistrust, is too sensitive. This manifests itself variously as anxiety and guilt, and as a terrible inability to be genuine and innocent, especially in the love of other people. The more penetrating one's self-awareness, the more it seems that life is a desperately elaborate game of one-upmanship, in which one pursues one's own selfish purposes under the many disguises of duty, love, public-spiritedness, and devotion to ideals.

Christianity presents itself as the response of God to this predicament, which is an "everlasting damnation" just because it is a vicious circle from which man cannot escape by his own efforts. And it presents itself in the form of a history—a history of those "mighty acts of God" which are recorded in the Bible. To summarize this history very briefly—as it is set out in the orthodox traditions—it began with a covenant between the Lord and an elect people, the Hebrews. No one really knows why, and perhaps the last word on this mystery remains, "How odd of God to choose the Jews." However, it was through this people and this culture, endowed, perhaps, with a peculiar genius for religion, that the Lord first revealed himself to the world through the Law and the Prophets.

The Law is set out in the Pentateuch, the first five books of the Bible, containing not only the Ten Commandments but the whole complex fabric of the Hebrew moral and ritual law. According to St. Paul, the Law was given to convict men of sin: to set before them the standards and ideals of perfection, so that they could see, not only how far short of them they were falling, but also that they had no power of their own to obey them. (See above, pp. 66–67.) Thus the Hebrews were perpetually falling short of the Law and consequently, as the Prophets explained, incurring the anger of God—visited upon them through the agency of Philistines, Amalekites, Assyrians, Babylonians, Seleucids, and Romans. But the message of the Prophets went considerably deeper than exhortations to obey the Law for fear of national disasters.

The Prophets insisted more and more on the idea that ritual observance of the Law was not enough, and that there could be no true obedience unless the Law was "written upon the heart"—that is, unless one desired genuinely to keep its precepts. Isaiah II went so far as to detach obedience from the hope of political success and material prosperity, trying to portray the ideal of Israel as the Suffering Servant, faithful to the ways of the Lord despite all the inevitable sufferings of this life, to be an example of pure unselfishness to the whole world.

However, the Prophets did not help anyone to get out of the vicious circle. Indeed, they made it much worse. For they showed that it was not enough to correct one's outward behavior; what God really demanded was the correction of the inner man, the conversion of the heart. And this is exactly what no one can do. It is completely blocked by the taint of Original Sin. As Luther put it:

> This understanding of the law spiritually is far more deadly, since it makes the law impossible to fulfill and thereby brings man to despair of his own strength, and abases him; for no one is without anger, no one without lust: such are we from birth. But what will a man do, when oppressed by such an impossible law? (9)

It was thus that, through the Law and the Prophets, the Lord brought about in perceptive hearts a sense of sin amounting almost to despair. This is certainly a revelation in the spirit of *upaya* or "holy cunning," to issue commandments, not expecting them at all to be obeyed, but to make men conscious of why they could not obey them.

According to Christianity, the solution of the problem lies in the mystery of the Incarnation and the Atonement—the birth, crucifixion, resurrection, and ascension of Christ. The Law and the Prophets had achieved nothing but despair and a certain degree of self-knowledge. The time was therefore ripe for a completely different kind of revelation, in the form, not of words, but of an *event* that would effect a radical change in human nature. The event was that God the Son, the archetypal pattern of the universe, became man, and the man was the historical Jesus of Nazareth. This is the absolute crux of all traditional Christianity: the faith that Jesus was infinitely more than a prophet, moralist, and exemplar—that he was God himself become human. The point was to bring into the world a Second Adam. The First Adam had, by his Fall, tainted all humanity with sin. The Second Adam would, by assuming man's birth, suffering, death, and burial, unite all humanity and all phases of human life with the divine nature. As St. Athanasius put it, "God became man that man might become God."

Theologians have made of this an extremely complex doctrine—trying to explain how "true God" could become "true man," and by what connections and channels the one man, Jesus, could achieve a transformation for all men. After all, how can God, the omnipotent and omniscient, become truly human —that is, capable of suffering, doubt, fear and sorrow —without ceasing to be God? As St. Paul put it:

> Let this consciousness be in you that was also in Christ Jesus, who [though] existing in the form of God, did not consider equality with God as some-

thing to be grasped; but, emptying himself, took the
form of a servant, and was born in the likeness of
men. And finding himself in fashion as a man, he
humbled himself and became obedient even to
death—the death of the cross. (*Philippians 2:* 5–8.)

God the Son, in other words, became man by "emptying himself," by a temporary setting aside or abandonment (*kenosis*) of the fullness of divine power.
God is, then, no longer in the position of watching
over the tribulations of men from a position of lordly
independence. He comes down and actually partici-
pates in all the limitations and sufferings of his own
creatures, including death by torture. Thereupon, the
extreme point of human humiliation—death—is peculiarly linked with the Godhead, and the vicious
circle of man's bondage is broken for all who will
accept the gift.

But how? How does the descent of God the Son
into one man affect all men? An ancient doctrine is
that his sacrifice of himself placated the wrath and
satisfied the justice of God the Father, so that the
latter consented to forgive all the sins that men had
committed and would commit. Most modern theologians feel that this is a rather primitive and blood-
thirsty explanation of the Atonement, as indeed it is
if the wrath of God is fundamentally serious. The preferred explanation is more complex, for it employs a
somewhat archaic method of reasoning derived from
Greek philosophy. When it is said that, in Jesus, God
became man, it does not say that he became *a* man.
Catholic doctrine insists that Jesus was not a human
person; he was a divine person, God the Son, but he
possessed, as well as his divine nature, a complete

human nature. For Greek thought distinguished between *nature* and *person*. The nature, whether human or divine, was the substance of Godhead or humanity; every divine or human person is an "hypostasis" of this substance, somewhat as ice, water and steam are hypostases of one substance. The definition of the person or hypostasis never attained any real clarity, and in any case the Latin *persona* (= mask) was an absurd translation of the Greek *hypostasis*. But the real point at issue is that in Jesus, God assumed the humanity, not of one man alone, but of all men. Figure out the *how* as you will, but this is definitely the *what*.

It follows, then, that the process of Incarnation—of uniting God and man—that began in Jesus is to extend from him so as to include, ultimately, the whole universe. This extending of the Incarnation is called the Body of Christ, otherwise known as the Church, and every human being can be made "one Body" with Christ by becoming baptized and accepting the faith that Jesus is God incarnate, with all that it implies. It should be mentioned in passing that most people confuse the Church with a building, or set of buildings, or with the clergy, whereas it has been well defined as "the blessed (i.e., happy) company of all faithful people." It is supposed to be God in the process of transfiguring the whole cosmos.

Christianity stresses the idea that salvation, or union with God, is a gift, and that the Incarnation is the sole means of this gift. There is absolutely no way of earning, deserving, or manufacturing salvation; it comes only as the grace, or favor, of God's love for man and the world. However, once this gift has been received, it is said to empower the individual to perform works "pleasing unto the Lord," and, further, that if such works do not emerge, the individual will be at fault for not appreciating the gift, and not making use of his divine talent.

Here we come right to the nub of the scheme. What does one do to receive *effective* grace, that is, grace that becomes fully realized in works of love? The problem is simply that innumerable people who have apparently fulfilled all the requirements—belief, prayer, reception of the sacraments, etc.—have found no significant change in their moral behavior, except, perhaps, a deeper duplicity than ever. St. Paul's statement of his dilemma while trying to follow the Law is as typical for a Christian as for a Jew: "The good that I would, I do not; but the evil that I would not, I do." If the problem for the Jew was to obey the Law, the problem for the Christian is to receive grace effectively—or to believe truly in Jesus. (It has been said that you believe in something when you behave as if it were true.) But are not these two problems the same? What more has Christianity to offer than Judaism if it is as hard to believe truly in Jesus as to do the works of the Law?

This problem arises so long as the test of truth and power in a religion is moral success. "By their fruits ye shall know them" is usually understood to mean that beliefs must be judged by their moral consequences, that they must issue in observance of the Ten Commandments, and in the various works of piety and mercy implied in the perfect love of God and of one's neighbor. Is there any way of demonstrating that Christians have achieved this goal more successfully than Jews—or than Muslims, Hindus, Buddhists, Parsees, Sikhs, and atheists? There is not, and it would show a serious lack of Christian humility to lay claims to superior righteousness. (Except that there is a very wicked morality game called, "I'm sorrier for my sins than you are.")

Now, is moral perfection, through divine grace, the actual goal of the Christian life? If St. Paul was right in supposing that the Lord delivered the Law to Moses, not expecting it to be obeyed, but to increase self-awareness and the conviction of sin, might not the dispensation of grace through the Incarnation have a similar purpose—perhaps at some deeper level? Theologians have always made a distinction between goodness and holiness, holding that the latter rather than the former is the Christian objective. Holiness, however, is usually taken to include goodness or, at least, a vigorous effort to attain it even if quite unsuccessful. Holiness is very hard to describe, but quite unmistakable when met with in the flesh: a wise innocence, a relaxed intensity, a humorous humility, a supernatural naturalness, an unsentimental devotion—all wrapped up in an atmosphere which is vaguely scary. For the holy man is numinous; he radiates something of the *shekinah*, the light of glory, the presence of the Most High.

Obviously, moral perfection through grace must be the *official* ideal of the Church, just as justification through obedience to the Law is the official ideal of the Synagogue. But the frequent testimony of those who follow, or try to follow, this ideal consistently is that it functions more as an *upaya*, as a means of grace, than as a goal. Here is Dom John Chapman, a late Abbot of Downside, writing to a nun:

> Do not exhaust yourself by making *efforts*. You seem still to think that you can make yourself good! You can't. But God can, and will; though slowly, perhaps. . . . Try to be simply at His disposition, ready to be recollected or distracted as He wills; to feel good or to feel wicked (which is nearer to humility), to be wretched or consoled. I know the darkness is appalling sometimes;—but it is the only way of learning that we depend entirely on God, that we have nothing from ourselves, that even our love and desire of Him tends to be selfish. The "royal way of the Holy Cross" is the only way. But you will find out that the darkness is God Himself; the suffering is His nearness. (10)

In the presence of holiness, there is always the feeling that moral rectitude is not only a caricature of holiness, but is in some way off the point. It knows the words, but doesn't know the music. "And though I bestow all my goods to feed the poor, and though I give my body to be burned, and have not charity, it profiteth me nothing."

Holiness is close to, but not quite the same as, a return to innocence and to the life of spontaneous impulse. A. K. Coomaraswamy called it "a perpetual uncalculated life in the present." For holiness is the life of spontaneity and self-abandonment *with humor*, which includes the wisdom of serpents as well as the gentleness of doves, because humor is nothing other than perfect self-awareness. It is the delighted recognition of one's own absurdity, and a loving cynicism with respect to one's own pretensions. A person who has learned to be *fully* self-aware can safely return to living by impulse. Humor is the transformation of anxiety into laughter: the same trembling, but with a different meaning. Holy humor is the discovery of the ultimate joke on oneself, and this is why Dante heard the song of the angels as the laughter of the universe.

I think of the crypt of the Capuchin Church on the Via Veneto in Rome: three chapels entirely decorated with the bones of the departed fathers. Altars made of piled skulls and shinbones; ceilings adorned with floral garlands, vertebrae for the flowers and ribs for the stems. Every fixture, every decoration—"dem bones." Hundreds of disassembled skeletons crammed into this small crypt with a narrow stairway. What an uproar there will be on the Day of Resurrection, when all those bones try to reassemble themselves and go scurrying upstairs for the Last Judgment! "Excuse me, father, but isn't that *my* fifth metatarsal?" When I saw the gently wicked glint in the eyes of the bearded little friar who was collecting the tourists' offerings, I realized that such chapels could have been created only by people who had completely seen through the terrors of death. Some dread skeletons; others play with them.

If, then, the actual living out of the Christian way seems to show that what lies at its end is something far beyond rectitude, that in holiness there is some secret gaiety; then it begins to look as if the dispensation of Grace might be as much an *upaya* as the dispensation of the Law. All is not apparent on the surface, for the Christian way embodies a fuller and deeper challenge to everything that man has supposed himself to be and has attempted to achieve since eating the forbidden fruit, and finding that he could no longer trust his impulses.

Yet this challenge can quite easily be overlooked, especially if the Lord God is taken to be just a solemn, literal-minded preacher. Taken that way, the message of Christianity boils down to something like this: After the Fall, no one could get into heaven, no matter how good they tried to be, because all their goodness was selfishly motivated. Then Jesus came. Because he was both God and man, he could act as and for man, yet at the same time he could act as God, with a motivation of the purest love. Thereupon he made a sacrifice of himself upon the cross which was tantamount to offering the whole of mankind to the Father, in a spirit of absolute unselfishness, and this sacrifice assured resurrection from death for all and likewise opened the gates of heaven to all. BUT —though the admission is now free, no one can find the entrance unless he genuinely believes that all this has happened, that the admission really *is* free, and then behaves as if it were true. What is more, as things now stand, you *must* believe, you *must* have faith—and the kind of behavior that goes with faith. Otherwise, the jaws of hell yawn for you.

The problem is therefore *how* to believe. For it is not enough to say that I believe, or that I would like to believe. "Not every one that saith unto me, Lord, Lord, shall enter into the kingdom of heaven; but he that doeth the will of my Father which is in heaven." How to have genuine faith is the same sort of problem as how to have genuine love, or how to ask sincerely for the grace to have them. Yet this is just what the Lord says I must have, for "Thou *shalt* love the Lord thy God." . . . "Darling, you must love your mother. But, of course, I want you to do it because *you* want to, and not because *I* say so." And what if I challenge my wife, and say, "Sweetheart, do you *really* love me?" and she replies, "Well, I'm trying my very best!" Is that the answer I want? You must do, quite deliberately, that which can only happen by itself. That seems to be the *real* first and greatest commandment.

Yet as soon as the self-contradictory pattern of the first and greatest commandment is seen, there comes a curious insight. The very sin of Adam was that he aspired to be as God—that is, to bend nature to his conscious will, to command spontaneous performances from himself and others! All technique—artistic, mechanical, dramatic, athletic, or medical—is the attempt to be skillfully natural or artfully artless, seeking to recapture and control, in human terms, the faultless grace of birds in flight. With rare exceptions, it succeeds at most in attaining a fair *imitation* of the ideal, concealing the laborious construction-work as on the underside of a piece of embroidery. But now it appears that the real intent of God's first and greatest commandment is to tell the sons of Adam to persist as hard as they can in that primal sin of trying to control spontaneity. Thou shalt love. Thou shalt be artificially natural. Thou shalt try not to try. Thou shalt willfully give up thine own will. Thou shalt attempt, for the next five minutes, *not* to think of a green elephant. Presumably, then, the Lord believes, with William Blake, that "the fool who persists in his folly will become wise."

If, therefore, this is the intent behind both the Law and the Incarnation, the whole history of Christianity is seen in a new and startling light. It becomes an immense success in persisting in folly! In going, full tilt, in a direction that must lead to a final coming to our senses. In perfecting the isolation and insularity of the human individual to its ultimate absurdity. In nurturing the feeling of personal responsibility and guilt to the point where it paralyzes action. For Christianity is one of the principal ingredients in the astonishing outburst of historical change which is so strangely characteristic of the West, in a cultural imperialism and a scientific sorcery which—in less than a hundred years—have won victories over nature which put the whole planet in peril.

This is not the place to elaborate on the lessons of ecology, the science of the interrelationships and balances of nature (11). The working of our merciful miracles of communication, medicine, sanitation, and nutrition has poisoned the soil and the atmosphere, infected the waters, dangerously disorganized all insects and micro-organisms, deprived food of taste, spread the insanities of nationalism and military technology to the ends of the earth, and made people their own worst enemy by a multiplication of their numbers which is out of all foreseeable control. Are not these the fruits of the Hebrew and Christian conviction that death is an evil, because I am all that there is of me, because, for all the hopes of heaven, death heralds the day of reckoning, the confrontation of me with my Maker in the supremely grim moment of the Last Judgment?

The folklore of death in the Christian West is a

compound of ghastliness—of the gloom of black mourning, of churchyards haunted with shrieking skulls, of dark coffins draped in sable, of ghosts with rattling bones robed in shrouds, of weird and dismal associations of black Bibles, bats and booming bells, of horribly avuncular undertakers with low voices, of kindly physicians and surgeons believing so strongly in "while there is life there is hope" that the pangs of death are interminably prolonged, and suicide deemed a mortal sin. When the sense of personal identity is most intensely developed, even the horrors of the Last Judgment and Hell are better than the prospect of everlasting nothingness. This is John Betjeman's feeling, lying in hospital before an operation, and listening to the Sunday evening bells.

> Swing up! and give me hope of life,
> Swing down! and plunge the surgeon's knife.
> I, breathing for a moment, see
> Death wing himself away from me
> And think, as on this bed I lie,
> Is it extinction when I die?
> I move my limbs and use my sight;
> Not yet, thank God, not yet the Night.
> Oh better far those echoing hells
> Half-threaten'd in the pealing bells
> Than that this "I" should cease to be—
> Come quickly, Lord, come quick to me. (12)

Individual life is deemed supremely valuable and important, and therefore death, despite all promises of eternal beatitude beyond the grave, is to be put off by all possible ingenuity. Remember Lazarus.

> Are not two sparrows sold for a farthing? and one of them shall not fall to the ground without your Father [knowing it]. But the very hairs of your

head are all numbered. Fear ye not therefore, ye are of more value than many sparrows. (*Matthew* 10: 29–31. AV.)

The fascinating paradox of Christianity is that this marvelously creative vision of the value of the individual can also be the undoing of the individual, and of human society as a whole. It is too much of a good thing. At the same time, we must not write off the Christian sense of personality as a mistake, to be replaced by some merely barbarous concept of the individual as "hand," "worker," "consumer," or other type of socialized digit. The explosion of Christian personality through its own intensity leads to something far better.

Meanwhile, the terrifying dislocations which are bearing down upon us as the result of a technology unmindful of ecology, compel us to ask some extremely radical questions. Is the attempt to master nature really worth it, in the long run? Is language and communication actually of help in survival? Will it soon be necessary to abandon the practice of medicine? Is government anything at root but an elaborate system of self-frustration? Are the ego and the power of conscious reason nothing but cumbersome clowns in comparison with the organic and paraconscious wisdom of the body? Are plagues and diseases our friends, keeping population at an optimal balance? Is the sense of individuality an illusion, the result of some curious disintegration and fixation of a racial, or even universal, consciousness? Are those in power soon going to be forced to select whole groups of people for painless extermination or sterilization? Should anyone try to control this mounting confusion, or simply relax and let things take their course? And then, could any of us really let go, even if it seemed the best thing to do?

Such questions have been asked before, but never with the earnestness that events will soon force upon us. How can they be answered by the type of man who has brought these problems about? Faced with this crisis, the egocentric style of personality will merely turn brutal, and there will be a frightful struggle for the survival of some elite group. The infinitely judicious combination of doing nothing and interfering intelligently that will be required, calls for human beings with a new sensation of identity. And this new sensation of identity could come about within the framework of Christianity, *if* Christians understood the way in which their religion works—as an *upaya*, as a systematic and formidably consistent egocentricity designed to explode into theocentricity—the realization of being one Self with God. Jesus put it in the plainest language:

> [I pray] that all may be one, *even as* you, Father, [are] in me and I in you, that they also may be in us, [and] that the world may believe that you have sent me. And I have given them the glory which you gave to me, that they may be one *just as* we are one—I in them and you in me—so that all may be completely in unity. (*John* 17: 21–23.)

The phrase "just as" or "even as" ($\kappa\alpha\theta\tilde{\omega}s$) leaves no doubt that he envisaged men becoming one with God in just the same way and degree as himself.

A system of consistent egocentricity? Christianity is always assumed to be the exact opposite, since it is so firmly opposed, say, to the gratification of sensual appetites without regard for other people. But that is a weak form of egocentricity—even, in extreme forms, a parody or inversion of a saint's love for God, since the deity here is sex or booze or chocolate cream pies. Strong egocentricity is a product of effort and discipline, and tends to make the individual feel that he is a separate, independent and responsible being, exercising an increasing degree of control over his environment, his physical organism and his own soul. St. Paul, who spoke so much of divine grace and of the obsolescence of the Law, could nevertheless write, "But I beat down my body, and bring it into subjection."

By and large, Christianity is the religion of grace much more in theory than in practice. It has been said, "Pray as if everything depended upon God, but work as if everything depended upon you." In other words, believe as if you had been given salvation, but behave as if you had to attain it by your own effort. Christian institutions—monasteries, convents, schools —have almost always been disciplinary mills, having long schedules of minute rules concerning speech, deportment, moral behavior, ritual observance, and even inward thoughts; and, during hundreds of years, the general practice has been to implement the comforting (i.e., energizing) grace of the Holy Spirit with the whip. To read through the ancient fathers of the Church, the medieval penitentiaries, the great sixteenth- and seventeenth-century manuals of ascetic theology and spiritual direction, is to see beyond doubt how consistently the Christian way has been an unceasing and critical watchfulness over the formation of personal character, to compel oneself by grace or by guts to conform in thought, word and deed to the pattern of Christ.[1]

Out of this ordinary (i.e., regular) discipline of the "purgative way," a few souls seem to graduate with the understanding that disciplinary success is not enough, and may even be the occasion of a frightful downfall. I may be able to control my passions and appetites, but in what spirit am I controlling them? Is it, after all, to admire myself for my moral strength, and not for any genuine love of God or of my brethren? With this insight, I know that somehow the spirit in which the discipline is followed must be changed. I must do all for the pure love of God, but I do not have the power to evoke such love by my own will. What am I to do, then? For I see that even in praying for the grace to love purely, I am trying to work some indirect magic, to find some trick, some psychic technique, some spiritual gimmick to compel the grace of God. How do I *not* want to do that?

This point is really the height of egocentricity: the final achievement of controlling my own letting go of myself; to be able to say "When!" To become the perfect instrument of the Spirit, and yet to have done it myself. To be able to evoke union with God at will —and, above all, by the stratagem of willing not to will it, for it seems to come just when I say, "O God, let it come or not come, as *you* will." (See Dom John Chapman's advice, above, p. 93.)

It is no wonder that, at this stage, I begin to feel

[1] There are other records which show the rule in the breach instead of the observance. But it would be safe to say that, for some 1900 years or more, a goodly majority of professing, church-going Christians have, at some time in their lives, at least made a stab at this task.

that drunkards, hipsters, bums, pimps and prostitutes are better than I, for at least they are straightforward and without pretensions. Jesus himself preferred to associate with such as these rather than with people aspiring to righteousness. (One must remember that the Pharisees were the "nice people" of those days, the decent and the law-abiding, the ladies and gentlemen.) So then—at this stage I feel to myself as if my hands were covered with molasses and feathers, and I were trying to pick the feathers off. I cannot possibly get myself out of my own way, for whatever I do or don't do, it is *I* that am doing it and it is *my* way. The situation is, in sum, that I *must* surrender myself, but I cannot possibly do so.

This is the apex of the discipline of self-consciousness, of the development of the Christian ego. It is reflected in the situation of Western civilization as a whole, for, on the one hand, we *must* let the balance of nature maintain itself, but, on the other, we are so dependent upon our technology that we cannot possibly abandon it.

At this point of crisis, what is the right question to ask? "What shall we do?" is clearly the wrong question, because we know we cannot do what must be done. The better question is, "What does it *mean* that we are in this crisis? What does our situation tell us about the way in which we have been acting, and about who or what we have believed ourselves to be?"

V

Who *Is* Who?

In what sense, then, is "Jesus Christ" the answer to this problem? Do his precepts and doctrines hold the solution? Or is it, as the Church insists, that *who* he was (and is) is still more important than what he said?

For the right Faith is, that we believe and confess: that our Lord Jesus Christ, the Son of God, is God, and Man; God of the substance of the Father, begotten before the worlds: and Man of the substance of his Mother, born in the world; Perfect God, and perfect Man: of a reasonable soul, and human flesh subsisting; equal to the Father, as touching his Godhead: and inferior to the Father, as touching his Manhood. Who although he be God and Man: yet he is not two, but one Christ; one, not by conversion of the Godhead into flesh, but by the taking of the Manhood into God; one altogether, not by confusion of substance, but by unity of person. For as the reasonable soul and flesh is one man: so God and Man is one Christ. (BCP.)

This, according to the so-called Athanasian Creed, is the heart of the matter. But how does it help? If one insists that God became man only in the year 753 *ab Urbe Condita*, from the founding of the city of Rome, and only within the skin of Jesus of Nazareth, this makes Jesus a freak with no effective relationship to other people. If Jesus had such a unique advantage over other men, it is merely a farce to suggest that they follow his example.

Does it help by guaranteeing that every word he said was the solemn, literal, and absolute truth, which we are therefore bound to believe? That 1900-odd years ago, he somehow settled a mysterious debt for me which I don't remember incurring? That everything he did was the perfect and finally authoritative example of conduct and morals—which we are expected to follow without the aforesaid advantage of being God the Son in person? That by some feat of ancient Greek logic, the Manhood of Jesus is also *my* Manhood, since Manhood is a universal "substance" which we all share in somewhat the same way as all pots share the substance of clay? But if this be so, Jesus has united me with God as touching my Manhood, my human nature, but *not* as touching my person—my particular form (or pot) of this substance. We are then back to the old, old problem of *how* my person, my will, my ego, my individual essence is to surrender itself to Christ's transformation of my substance.

On this point the doctrines are more and more complex, and less and less helpful. When God the Son became man, as Jesus of Nazareth, this effected a *potential* union of his humanity with mine. To clinch this union I must, however, be baptized, and then confirmed, and then be a regular recipient of the sacraments of penance and holy communion. Yet this does no more than to advance the union of my humanity with Christ's humanity from the potential level to the actual, and thus to make grace available to my person, my will, in the hope that this may enable me to take the essential leap of faith, of personal commitment to the gift of salvation vouchsafed to my humanity, to my impersonal and collective status as a human being. Remember that the substance (clay) is one thing and the person (the pot) another, and that therefore the gift of salvation to the substance is not the same thing as the salvation of the person. The former makes the latter possible. But, as we have seen, it is as difficult to co-operate personally with grace as to obey the precepts of the law with sincerity of heart. The gift of grace, of the union of my humanity with Christ, makes no difference; we are just where we were before.

The preceding paragraph contained a highly simplified account of *how* we are "saved"—or given the opportunity to be saved—through the Incarnation of God the Son as Jesus of Nazareth. But is it upon such quibbles and splittings of hair that the whole force of the Gospel must be supported? For all this is a symbology and a way of thinking quite strange to my life as a member of twentieth-century Western culture, and stranger still, for example, to university students in Ghana or Tokyo. It fails absolutely to make any direct connection between the crucified and risen Son of God, on the one hand, and the daily life of a family in the suburbs of Los Angeles or London, on the other.

Direct connections are made by the Billy Grahams, and other Bible-bangers, who simply bypass the problem of *how* the Crucifixion in A.D. 34 saves me in 1964, who just assume that it *does*, and then go on to convince me of the divine and noble character of Jesus as portrayed in the Bible, clinching the argument by saying that this is also the character of the God who supports and creates my existence at this very moment. They tell me that if I want to know what God is like, God who is the foundation of my being here and now, I must read about Jesus in the Gospels who is "the brightness of [God's] glory and the express image of his person." I can therefore communicate with the Power that supports me here and now on the assumption that it both resembles and, in some sense, *is* the historical Jesus of Nazareth, risen from the dead and reigning in heaven. I don't need to worry and ask questions about *how* Jesus will save me; I have only to pray, to communicate with him, and, to my utter surprise, I will find that the power to surrender myself is immediately forthcoming.

But if one happens to be blessed (or cursed) with a critical intellect, this simply will not do. One is then quick to see that the surrender of the will to Jesus is all too easily a blind acceptance of patriarchal mores and a return to the conscience of one's childhood. For Billy Graham's Jesus is an ideal image of the bourgeois Middle West, just as the Catholic Jesus is an ideal feudal prince of the thirteenth century, or a Boston-Irish male mother with a big worry about sex.

Christian piety makes a strange image of the object of its devotion, "Jesus Christ, and Him crucified." Him. The bearded moralist with the stern, kind, and vaguely hurt look in the eyes. The man with the lantern, knocking at the heart's door. "Come along now, boys! Enough of this horsing around! It's time you and I had a very serious talk." Christ Jesus our Lord. *Jeez*-us. Jeez-*you*. The Zen Buddhists say, "Wash out your mouth every time you say 'Buddha!'" The new life for Christianity begins just as soon as someone can get up in church and say, "Wash out your mouth every time you say 'Jesus!'"

For we are spiritually paralyzed by the fetish of Jesus. Even to atheists he is the supremely good man, the exemplar and moral authority with whom no one may disagree. Whatever our opinions, we must perforce wangle the words of Jesus to agree with them. Poor Jesus! If he had known how great an authority was to be projected upon him, he would never have said a word. His literary image in the Gospels has, through centuries of homage, become far more of an idol than anything graven in wood or stone, so that today the most genuinely reverent act of worship is to destroy that image. In his own words, "It is expedient for you that I go away, for if I go not away, the Paraclete (the Holy Spirit) cannot come unto you." Or, as the angel said to the disciples who came looking for the body of Jesus in the tomb, "Why do you seek the living among the dead? He is not here. He is risen and has gone before you. . . ." But Christian piety does not let him go away, and continues to seek the living Christ in the dead letter of the historical record. As he said to the Jews, "You search the scriptures, for in them you *think* you have eternal life."

The Crucifixion gives eternal life because it is the giving up of God as an object to be possessed, known, and held to for one's own safety, "for he that would save his soul shall lose it." To cling to Jesus is therefore to worship a Christ uncrucified, an idol instead of the living God.

> Rock of ages, cleft for me,
> Let me hide myself in thee.

The cockroaches run for their cracks in the wall.

> What a friend we have in Jesus,
> All our sins and griefs to bear!

But the Christ who "walks with me and talks with me" is not the Christ within; he is the crutch, not the backbone. The continuing Sacrifice of the Altar, the daily breaking and consuming of Christ's Body in the Mass, means nothing at all if it does not mean that the imagined Jesus and the preconceived God is always being surrendered—the shell shattered and the seed buried so that the life may be released. As Jesus said, "A grain of wheat remains a solitary grain unless it falls into the ground and dies; but if it dies, it bears a rich harvest." But the bystanders then, as the pious today, objected, "Our Law teaches us that the Messiah continues forever. What do you mean by saying

that the Son of Man must be lifted up [i.e., cruci-
fied]?" And thus:

> O Word of God incarnate,
>   O Wisdom from on high,
> O Truth, unchanged, unchanging,
>   O Light of our dark sky;
> We praise thee for the radiance
>   That from the hallowed page,
> A lantern to our footsteps,
>   Shines on from age to age

so that we all know exactly where we are.

Belief in a definite and objective Christ to be
leaned upon is, however, the antithesis of faith; it is
an attitude that is rigid rather than trusting and
yielding. Christian piety is notoriously preoccupied
with rigid images.

> Christ is made the sure foundation,
>   Christ the head and corner-stone.

Or, as Samuel Johnson put it:

> In vain the surge's angry shock,
>   In vain the drifting sands:
> Unharmed upon the eternal rock
>   The eternal city stands.

And Luther:

> A mighty fortress is our God,
>   A bulwark never failing.

But what we need in a universe such as ours are not
rocks and bastions: we need the knowledge of how to
float and swim. In the end, the pliability, the elastic-
ity, and the "give" of living tissue is always stronger
than stone and steel. Perhaps, then, the dolphins were
wiser than we, since they left the firm earth to romp

and roll in the oceans. We maintain the illusion of living in a solid world, though in fact a mountain range of granite is a diaphanous network of electrical energy, and the attitude of the dolphin is as appropriate on land as in the water.

To have faith in "Christ crucified" is therefore "that he may be *in* us, and we *in* him," as the bird is in the air and the air in the bird. It is not to cling to the Cross or to reach out in the dark for the Savior's hand. There is nothing to catch hold of, because "the kingdom of heaven is within you." To be truly "in Christ" is to be less and less preoccupied with any external image of Jesus derived from the Gospels, as if the Christian life were the meticulous following of a pattern. Every Easter Sunday should be celebrated with a solemn and reverent burning of the Holy Scriptures, for the whole meaning of the resurrection and ascension of Christ into heaven ("which is within you") is that Godmanhood is to be discovered here and now inwardly, not in the letter of the Bible.

This is why the quest for the historical Jesus is so dreary and unproductive. Our attempts to "demythologize" the Gospel (Bultmann) and get down to the authentic, historical facts about Jesus of Nazareth are actually as irrelevant and superstitious as trying to concoct pseudoscientific proofs that the Virgin Birth and the bodily Resurrection were physical events. Both are quests for a Jesus out there in the past, and "why seek ye the living among the dead?" Christ demythologized invariably turns out to be a rather boring prophet or messianic fanatic—at best a man struggling to express a profound experience of "cosmic consciousness" in the terms of Isaiah II's messianism and of post-Maccabean apocalyptic visions of the coming end of the world, a theology strangely alien to the mystical sense of union with God.[1] The various versions of the historical Jesus always seem to reflect the individual scholar's preconceptions of what Jesus ought to have said and done, and thus there is a curious disagreement among the "higher critics" as to what parts of the Gospels should be considered authentic. The historical Jesus may be an academic curiosity; he is hardly the object of a spiritual quest, and scholarly attempts to dig out the hard facts from the poetry and mythology of the Gospels are somewhat similar to explorations of Mozart's sonatas in terms of the physics of sound.

Is it really of any great interest to ask whether Jesus was literally and historically born of a virgin and resurrected physically after his death? This kind of emphasis makes him a human freak, like a two-headed baby. The marvel of marvelous events is not whether they happened but what they mean, and the wonder of mythological happenings is that their meaning is almost inexhaustible. Like magic mirrors, every man can see in them the truth that is right for him and for his time. The *meaning* of the miracle is as important for the age which takes miracles for granted, as for the age which takes them with skepti-

[1] If Jesus had had a very strong form of the common type of "cosmic consciousness" in which the individual feels that his own inmost Self, behind the superficial ego, is God, this would have been almost impossible to express in terms of Judaic theology without blasphemy. The best he could have done was to identify himself, publicly, with the orthodox image of the promised Messiah, both as Isaiah II's Suffering Servant and as the apocalyptic Son of Man, coming to rule the earth with the power of heaven rather than force of arms.

cism; in either age, the *fact* of the miracle is of no great consequence. It is only by the transposition of the miracle from historical and terrestrial time to mythological and celestial time that we can find:

> Christ walking on the water, not of Gennesareth but Thames!

Only if Bethlehem (the "House of Bread") becomes the human body, does it mean anything to sing

> O holy Child of Bethlehem!
> Descend to us we pray;
> Cast out our sin and enter in,
> Be born in us today.

Only if the Last Supper is set free from being an event long passed in Jerusalem is it possible for Christ to celebrate Mass with us today. If the Sacrifice "that bought us, once for all, on Calvary's tree" happened only on the fourteenth day of Nisan in A.D. 34, the answer to "Were you there when they crucified my Lord?" is merely, "No." And it was just nonsense for Johann Heermann to write:

> 'Twas I, Lord Jesus, I it was denied thee:
> I crucified thee.

Safely tucked away in ancient history, or off in some improbable local heaven, Christ can never be the beggar that comes to the door; and it was nothing more than a figure of speech when he said, "Inasmuch as you have done it unto one of the least of these my brethren, you have done it unto me."

To insist on the historicity of the Christian myth is to remove Christ to the sterile distance of an archaeological curiosity. Actually, this is a relatively modern point of view. It was not until 1700, or later, that Christian artists attempted to dress Jesus and his apostles with the historical realism of burnooses. They were always shown in the dress of the artist's day, or in the ecclesiastical vestments of the day. If we were now following the spirit of traditional Christian art, we would show Jesus in overalls or a tweed suit. It was taken for granted that the Gospels told of historical events, but that aspect of the matter was of minor importance. The important thing was that through the cycle of the Church year, and through the daily celebration of the liturgy, these marvelous and saving events were constantly relived in the present. They were not merely memorialized. They were mysteries in which men partook immediately, and this is still the basic attitude of Catholic spirituality. The notion that Christianity is the uniquely historical religion, stressing the intervention of God in the historical process, hardly occurred to theologians before the nineteenth century. But it was just at this time that Christianity also began to cultivate a pious antiquarianism, now culminating in the sentimentality of building Romanesque churches in steel and concrete. And watch out for plastic Baroque.

It is also in quite modern times that clergy have developed the attitude that there is something robust and realistic in committing oneself to the belief that, say, the virgin birth was a "hard, historical fact." This kind of commitment is contrasted with the alleged wooliness and feeble-mindedness of understanding it in the "impoverished" sense of "mere" myth or symbol. Obviously, such attitudes are a form of professional posturing which attempt to justify obscurantism and intellectual barbarism. It is in the same kind of spirit that some people acquire a sense of pragmatic manliness by adopting fascistic and "damn-it-shoot-'em-all" attitudes in politics.

We return, then, to the original question: in what sense is Jesus Christ "the answer" to our human predicament today? What relevance has this mighty mythos to men who feel themselves alone in an alien universe, trapped by their own ingenuity into being compelled to control a situation which thereby gets more and more out of hand? Clearly, he has no relevance as a practical preacher, giving straightforward, down-to-earth instructions which we have simply to put into practice. Still less is he relevant as a *deus ex machina,* a supernatural escape from all these problems, who, if we trust him to do so, will restore us to perfection and happiness after we are dead.

In the first place, the figure of Jesus—as passed down to us by orthodox tradition—is a challenge that no Westerner can simply dismiss, especially if he was exposed to it in childhood, and, quite as especially, if he was brought up as a Jew.[2] Directly or indirectly, the traditional image of Jesus has formed the personality, the sense of identity, and the scale of values of every member of Western culture. Even those of us who are downright irreligious find that there is still enough magic in his Name for effective cursing.

The difficulty is, however, that the Christian and Western style of personality is still half-baked, for it

[2] A major part of the Western Jew's problem is that he has to live with Christians, and thus cannot simply ignore the crucial differences between Christianity and Judaism. His tradition is still repressing the question of why Jesus was handed over to Pilate, and there can be no peace for him until he faces it.

expresses the unsolved problem which Christ himself posed in the double-bind commandment, "Thou *shalt* love the Lord thy God." You *must* be free. You are responsible for the deliberate cultivation of *genuine* concern and love for other people. We are thus trying to be human on purpose, as if we felt it necessary to go around making great efforts to have heads. Still more embarrassing, Jesus is saying, "I have suffered the agonies of the Cross because I loved you, and died to save you from your sins. Now what are you going to do for me?" Every Good Friday our parish clergy used to hand each one of us a colored picture of a very sad Jesus on the Cross, saying:

> This I have done for thee.
> What doest thou for Me?

Because of the Fall, you are guilty just for existing. But now that you have been redeemed at so great a price, you should be feeling absolutely terrible. And thus our parents, too, learned to make a play for our love by harping on the great sacrifices they made for us.

("It's not enough to *say* that you're sorry. Are you *really* sorry? No, don't try to tell me anything; we'll see clearly enough from your actions. And I don't mean from an outburst of penitence during the next few days. We'll have to see how you behave over a considerable period of time. . . .")

> O my people, what have I done unto thee?
> or in what have I afflicted thee? answer me.
> Because I led thee out of the land of Egypt,
> thou hast prepared a Cross for thy Savior.
> I gave thee a royal scepter, and thou hast
> given me a crown of thorns.

Is it nothing to you, all ye that pass by?
behold, and see if there be any sorrow like unto
my sorrow.

The God-Man on the Cross sums up in one image
all the cruelty we inflict by being alive, all the ravages of human selfishness and thoughtlessness. This
is why Jesus cannot be overlooked or dismissed. But
what is anyone to do? I can weep and beat my breast,
and devote the rest of my life to working as a medical
missionary, accepting contributions from stockholders
in missile factories, and using drugs supplied by firms
that fleece the public with dubious or dangerous pills.
Will it be all right if I don't *know* about it? I can look
on with a sort of passive despair, regretfully recognizing that I can never meet the challenge, and must
just muddle along as harmlessly as possible. Or I can
tell the Lord off, and say, "Listen, don't pull that stuff
on me! After all, you're supposed to be God. You
made me and you made the world this way, and if
you don't like the way I act it's up to *you* to change
it."

But, again, if I am sensitive and concerned, and if
I have a critical intellect, none of these responses will
do. I begin slowly to see that the challenge and the
problem of the God-Man on the Cross is not simply
something that I am looking at, out there. The more
conscious of myself I become, the more I realize that
I too am hanging on that same Cross. It will be just
as painful as crucifixion to die of stomach cancer, or
to be the helpless cause of suffering to people I love,
or to become all-too-vividly aware of my complicity
in the collective deviltries of our society. Crucifixion
is acute consciousness. At this level of understanding,

Jesus begins to disappear as a conventional image. There is no more the earnest young man with a beard and a white robe, or even the twisted body nailed to the beams. This image vanishes into the experience of suffering as such—not only physical pain, but also the empty aridity of "My God, my God, why hast thou forsaken me?" I see the crucifix when I swat a mosquito or eat an oyster, and how much more in all encounters with human pain. Yet the most problematic form of this crucifixion is in the insistent question, "What am I to *do* about it?"

Every response I can imagine is phony—even to confess that I am phony all the way through. As Groddeck once pointed out, there is still something a little bit pharisaical about the publican in the parable who creeps into the back of the temple and, beating his breast, cries, "God be merciful to me a sinner!" Once the story has been told and set up as an example, it becomes simply impossible to follow the example without falling into ever deeper entanglements of hypocrisy. Which is surely why Jesus told it. For once even the most genuine humility is held up for our emulation, its following is as hollow as the most perfunctory ritual.[3] So what *am* I to do?

I said to my soul, be still, and wait without hope
For hope would be hope for the wrong thing; wait
   without love
For love would be love of the wrong thing; there is yet
   faith

[3] Compare also the precept-shattering precept, "You have learned that they were told, 'Do not commit adultery.' But what I tell you is this: If a man looks on a woman with a lustful eye, he has already committed adultery with her in his heart." (*Matthew* 5: 27–28. NEB.)

But the faith and the love and the hope are all in the
  waiting.
Wait without thought, for you are not yet ready for
  thought:
So the darkness shall be light, and the stillness the
  dancing. (13)

But can I even wait, can I even *not* do, without being
just as much of a sham as ever?

The tradition of Western mysticism is that contemplative prayer, the highest knowledge of God attainable in this life, is the mute enduring of this
humiliating incapacity to hope for or to love the right
thing. Contemplative prayer is simply the faith that
this sense of incapacity is an interior crucifixion
whereby we come most immediately into union with
God. The vision of God in light and face-to-face must
wait until after death. Until then, the most perfect
knowledge of God is in the way of the Cross—in
knowing that one does *not* know God, in desolation of
spirit, in aridity, in feeling perfectly ordinary and
boringly everyday—in the faith that just this darkness
is the veiled Godhead. "Had I a God whom I could
understand," said Eckhart, "I would no longer hold
him for God." To quote Dom John Chapman again:

Your *prayer* will consist in passing the time as
best you can—as far as possible by simply belonging to God, without acts [i.e., specific acts of devo-
tion]—[or] using acts to avoid distractions. At the
end (and all through) you will be thanking God for
giving you *this particular prayer* and no other; it
will probably consist of (i) only distractions and
worrying; or (ii) nothing at all; or (iii) utter misery, and feelings of despair; or (iv) that there is no
God; or (v) that it is all dreadful, and waste of time

and pain. And you will then (not at once) feel—in a higher part of the soul than you have realized before—how much better this is than what you used to have; and that you would rather suffer like this, as it is God's will, than to have the most spiritual of pleasures. (14)

It is here, as Dom Aelred Graham (another Benedictine) has suggested, that Western mysticism has a certain affinity with Zen Buddhism, for Zen discovers the highest illuminantion, not in visions and ecstasies, but in the immediate here and now, as when the meaning of the universe is realized in "the clatter of a broken tile." It was in reference to this boring everydayness that the Zen master Bokuju was asked, "We have to dress and eat every day, and how do we escape from these chores?" He answered, "We dress; we eat." But the inquirer replied, "I don't get the point." "If you don't get it," said Bokuju, "put on your clothes and eat your food." Was this what George Herbert had in mind?

> All may of thee partake;
> Nothing can be so mean,
> Which with this tincture, "for thy sake,"
> Will not grow bright and clean.
>
> A servant with this clause
> Makes drudgery divine:
> Who sweeps a room, as for thy laws,
> Makes that and the action fine.

Not quite. There is in both Dom John's and Herbert's feeling a touch of spiritual masochism, not, by any means, as something to be deplored, but as something on the verge of a still greater understanding.

How very good all this suffering is for me! There is a certain wonderfully inverted security in being able to feel that, come what may, I am all right so long as I hurt.

> Oh! I bless the good Lord for my Boils,
>> For my mental and bodily pains,
> For without them my Faith all congeals
>> And I'm doomed to Hell's ne'er-ending Flames. (15)

A person in this state should soon see that he chooses a false security, that this comfort in suffering is the last resort of the hopelessly trapped ego, trying desperately to find a way of DOING THE RIGHT THING. Desperate it is. Not only is activism wrong: there is no right thing to do. Quietism is also wrong: there is nothing not to do, for *not* doing is just as much in the trap as doing.

If, at this extreme point, "Jesus Christ" is still "the answer," what can that mean? What does it mean to *be* at this point? What have I found out about myself when I see that neither my doing nor my not-doing is the answer? If I have found out that I cannot do the one and only thing that really needs to be done, what then?

To repeat the problem: I cannot avoid the challenge of the Crucifixion, for it means that just in being alive I am unavoidably responsible for untold misery and pain. Apologies are hollow. Attempts at improvement create new entanglements. Passivity is simple evasion.

The meaning is that what I thought was myself was a phantom. My ego was never an effective agent. My supposed controlling of the world and of myself was a Big Act—like a child sitting beside the driver of a car, getting the feel of guiding it himself with a toy steering-wheel. But then, who or what am I? If I can neither do nor not do, still, at least, I *know*. I am aware. Am I simply some sort of passive mirror which merely reflects experience? *Who* is it that knows? Look as I may, I find no knower—only knowing; no doer—only doing. Yet all this is somehow encompassed in that odd sensation of centrality which I call "I." And I know that *you* feel just as central and just as much "I" as I myself. I know, too, that when in sleep or in death the centrality which I presume to call mine vanishes, there remain myriads of other centralities, all of whom are as much "I" as I am. Thus when I die, there is no positive nonexistence to be experienced and endured, no state of being shut up in darkness forever. That is quite the most absurd bugbear that ever oppressed man's imagination. Beyond every death there is simply "I" again somewhere else, as there was when I was born. For "*I* am the vine, and you are the branches." "*I* am the way and the truth and the life." "Before Abraham was, *I* am."

"*I* and the Father are one!" Again the Jews picked up stones to stone him. Jesus answered them, "I have shown you many good works from the Father. For which of these works do you stone me?" The Jews replied to him, "We do not stone you for a good work but for blasphemy, and because you, being a man, make yourself God." Jesus answered them, "Isn't it written in your Law that 'I have said: you are gods'? If he called those [people] gods to whom the word of God came (and the scripture cannot be broken), how can you say to him whom the Father has made holy and sent into the world,

'You blaspheme!' because I said, 'I am a son of God'?" (*John* 10: 30–36.)[4]

The point is that identity is God. The expression "son of" means "of the nature of" or "of the essence of," as also, derogatively, in "son of a dog," "son of Belial," or "son of perdition." In this sense also we can understand Isaiah II's, "That they may know from the rising of the sun, and from the West, that there is none beside me. I am the Lord, and there is none else." So, too, the Islamic Sufis say of Allah, "As there is no Deity but he, so there is no Heity but he." This is likewise the point of St. Paul's, "I am crucified with Christ. Nevertheless I live; yet no more I, but Christ lives in me." And St. Catherine of Genoa, "My *me* is my God: nor do I know any selfhood except in God." The ultimate shock of realizing Who *is* who comes only at the point where my supposed personal self is seen to be nothing. (Not *bad* nothing, but a marvelous mirage.) Then, on the principle of St. Paul's "as having nothing but possessing all things," the nothing is seen to be the same as the All, the void the same as the Plenum. God emptying himself to the limit is man, and man emptied to the limit is God. Thus to be *in* Christ, to be One Body with him, to be in union with the Word made flesh, and to be partakers of his flesh and blood, is just to realize one identity with him who is "I am" before Abraham *was*.

[4] This is as literal a translation of the Greek as I can make of this crucial passage. The quotation from the Law is Psalm 82, "I have said, You [are] gods; and all of you [are] children of the Most High. But you shall die like men, and fall like one of the princes." The AV, without justification in the Greek, translates the final phrase, "I am *the* Son of God," the italic *the* signifying interpolation by the translators. The NEB skips the issue with, "I am God's son."

(Now, in introducing what follows, may I say that I write in the first person because there is no fairer way of being direct. The stilted "one feels" lacks commitment, and the editorial "we" evokes a false authority. "It would seem that" is impossibly pedantic. Also, I am using the conventional phrases of scripture and liturgy to speak a common language with those who inherit the Christian tradition.)

Having thought this question of identity through for years and years, I see no better way to make sense of it. The more I plumb the depths of myself, the more they seem to be beyond me, if "me" is no more than my superficial consciousness. But those depths are a dimension of myself not usually recognized. I can think and think about the mortality of my separate organism: what will it be like to go to sleep and *never* wake up? Yet this inevitably makes me think of my birth, of waking up after having never gone to sleep! Who would I have been as my mother's child by some other father? Of course, it is so startlingly obvious: I *could* have been anyone, but the only way to be anyone is to be someone. I am always someone, but "I" is ordinarily experienced only as being some-one-at-a-time. All sentient beings, wheresoever located in our multitudes of galaxies, are each "I."

Whatever there is of "I" beyond, beneath, or above the small spotlit circle of the ego goes its own way like the circulation of the blood and the formation of the bones. It is all done without conscious attention; and so, in exactly the same way, the everlasting recurrence of the I-feeling is maintained through the whole body of the universe. For as flocks of birds and clusters of cells or molecules move as if they had a single mind, so the conscious ego belongs in a universal Self. My centrality and identity is always a special case (a spotlit circle) of the centrality and identity of that Self. And it—the universal Self—can appear as "I" after "I" without the least need for any conscious memory of continuity, just as we need no conscious memory of how to breathe. Being all that there is, there is no standpoint outside this Self from which it can be observed. It has no more need to be a known object than a finger to touch itself or an eye to see itself.

Simply, then, the real "I" both in and beyond the spotlit circle, both in consciousness and beyond consciousness, is nothing less than all that there is. Obviously, I exist only *in relation* to everything else, but I did not *come into* that relation from somewhere outside—in such a way that "everything else" would be foreign to or other than myself. I did not alight in this universe like a bird arriving upon a branch from some alien limbo. I grew upon that branch like a leaf. For I am something which everything is doing; I am the whole process waving a flag named me, and calling out, "Yoo-hoo!"

I have, then, no further need to be anxious for myself. (Not, at any rate, far deep down.) For in the cosmological game of hide-and-seek I am "It." So I am let go: there can be endless appearances, reappearances, forgettings, vanishings, annihilations, transformations, total blackouts, and sudden explosions into light out of nowhere. There is no *need* to remember, for, in whatever form, it is always "I" who am there, the mercy of death delivering me again and again from the tedium of immortality. Equally, there is no need to cling to or believe in this fundamental and eternal "I am." For it is what there is: before it, there is no before; after it, no after; and outside it, no outside.

In slightly differing forms, this is one of the world's most ancient and perennial intuitions. It is madness and megalomania only if the Self of all selves is conceived in the image of a Chaldean or Iranian King of kings who deliberately rules the kingdom with armed and conscious might. For centuries Western man has thought upon God in this regal image, and has therefore come to feel himself a subject and serf, an alien and outsider in the universe. When, therefore, we arrive in the world as children, we are not given a frank and open welcome. We are not treated as if we, also, were people—handicapped, it may be, with infancy, but with the right to a fair explanation of the rules of the game as adults play it. On the contrary, the child is treated as if the limitations of infancy were a sin, as if childhood were an obsequious novitiate, a state of petitioning for human nature, of evolutionary probation and sufferance. Raised in this atmosphere, children never cease to feel that this is a world in which they do not really belong. Thus educated, men go through life on tiptoe, ever fearing to offend the mysterious Authority behind things, and the claim to be one Self with the eternal Ground of the world is felt to be the ultimate impertinence and effrontery.

Christianity does not have to remain in this nursery and boarding-school atmosphere. But it is not as if we were all grown up enough to be disagreeably authoritarian in our own right, as if we were entering into a New Age in which all Christians were entitled to assume the manners of an archbishop. It is rather that we are in a position to see that this whole image of the universe as an imperial and monarchical state is a joke. The Lord putting on crowns and beards and suits of celestial armor and panoplies of spiritual war to impress himself in the mirror. The ultimate identity of man with God is not identity with this Commander-in-Chief of the universe.

Serious theologians do not, of course, take such royal and military symbolism literally, though it probably influences their emotional attitudes more than they suspect. On the one hand, they can speak of God as an entirely beardless Spirit "without body, parts, or passions," as the "Circle whose center is everywhere and whose circumference is nowhere," and as "the love that moves the sun and other stars." Yet on the other hand they will also cluck about how grievously "our very dear Lord" is offended by fornication and profane language, as if the kingdom of heaven were something like the court of Queen Victoria. It is a complex type of mind that reads Jacques Maritain or William Temple, and gets a heart-throb from singing "Onward Christian Soldiers" in procession.

Theology balks at the proposition "identity is God" because it stresses the value of a multitude of unique and irreducible identities, that is, of *persons* under the rule and judgment of a Lord who is ultrapersonal and who constitutes a unique *integrity* in its double sense of individual unity and inflexible righteousness. Theology emphasizes the God who takes a clear stand, who will not be bribed or wheedled, and whose outlines—or principles—will not be blurred by any pantheistic merging with the universe. Any fuzzing of the distinction between God's identity and all other identities makes God an accessory to the manifest sinfulness of the human world. This God is God just because he cannot be manipulated and pushed around. He stands for his own vision of universal order without any compromise, and will make no concessions for the sake of being a good fellow and getting along with others.

All this is fine so long as we are playing the Christian game in which the primal conspiracy between the Lord and the Devil is suppressed. The trouble is that it gets suppressed completely, because the theology of the righteous God does not seem to be able to have its way without having to have it all the way. It must maintain the distinction between Creator and creature, as between good and evil, right down to the bitter end—which is, indeed, very bitter. But it should surely be possible to hold that a distinction is most important without having to make it absolutely important. A song is not worthless because it comes to an end, and a difference between the Creator and the creature is not negligible if it is not continued down to the root and ground of Being. Are the differences between a tree's branches annulled because they join in the trunk? Are my fingers less agile for being one with the hand? . . . It should be possible, too, to accept and follow the rules of a game (e.g., language or banking) without identifying them with the laws of either heaven or nature, and, likewise, to have decent and law-abiding behavior in any given community without having to invoke the authority and the sanctions of Infinity.

To carry the problems of morality before the Court of Heaven is not unlike trying to settle international disputes with nuclear bombs. The apocalyptic violence of Hell-fire is a threat which has done little or nothing to promote righteousness and diminish wickedness, for, like the H-bomb, it is inconceivable and unthinkable, and tends, as do judicial torture and capital punishment, to bring authority into disrespect. (It will be jolly, won't it, to be sitting around making music with the angels, knowing that your daughter is meanwhile screaming in the everlasting dungeons?) It makes no difference to say that it is not God who inflicts this punishment, but the individual forcing it upon himself in willful rejection of God's love; that the fire of Hell is the Light of Glory as apprehended by one who willfully spurns it. The point is that a universe involving this as a serious possibility is a monstrous misconstruction from the beginning.

Yet once we have reached the point of view at which all identity is God (*tat tvam asi*), we can see that behind this theological nightmare there is the fascination of a supernal masochism. Behind the façade of the terror and guilt, the fantasies of orgiastic torture prolonged forever without destroying the body, and the emotional convulsions of total despair, there is at last man's eternal preoccupation with ecstasy. The fascination, the positive attraction of these horrors is—in psychiatric language—unconscious, or better, unadmitted, as one does not admit a secret delight in grief or hatred or in being a professional failure. All such fascinations are ordinarily considered morbid and pathological, though this is only to say that in our "normal" consciouness we daren't admit that they are fascinating. Yet it is obvious that life, as a self-eating system of organisms, "wills" pain as much as it wills pleasure. It follows, then, that a master of life is one who admits or becomes conscious of his own secret preoccupation with ecstasy in the form of pain—but not as self-punishment, not as the last desperate attempt to placate the Father by "doing the right thing." If, as many of the mystics have said, the Cross is the heart of the universe, the meaning is not that God loathes himself; it is that the Indestructible dares all extremes. Higher than, and behind, the groveling masochism of "I bless the good Lord for my Boils" and of "How good all this suffering is for me," there is the mysterious point where extreme love and extreme pain are identical. I say "mysterious" because the ambivalence of pleasure and pain is one of the least studied problems of physiology, psychology, and esthetics. Mysterious, also, because it lies in the dangerous and touchy realm of all that we know and will not admit, the domain of our being that we deny most angrily when others point to it.

The orthodox and conventional Christian has therefore a remarkable choice before him: If he will not admit this secret fascination with pain as ecstasy, that all outward human agony is inwardly the divine in the act of self-abandonment, he must settle for real, vindictive, and finally evil hells whose very existence, however remote in the outer darknesses, must throw gloom into the joy of heaven. Or would he care to join a communion of saints who, as I believe even St. Thomas suggested, will look over the battlements of heaven and lick their lips with satisfaction at the just punishments of the damned?

In sum, then, the inner sense of the faith that salvation somehow consists in "Jesus Christ and him crucified" is that this mighty image shatters and transforms our sense of identity. So long as we insist on our separate, individual identity the Crucifixion is an impossibly burdensome scandal about which we can do neither something nor nothing. Yet this very frustration is already being "crucified with Christ," already the realization that our "I'm-just-poor-little-me" identity is an illusion. Coupled with the impossible commandment, "Thou *shalt* love the Lord thy God," this crucifixion carries the sense of separate individuality and conscious will-power to a critical, and absurd, extreme—at which point the illusion explodes into the discovery of our original and eternal Identity.

Thereupon it becomes possible to see that our fall, our adventure into separate individuality, comes to an end in the same way that it began—by the mystery of Sacrifice, of *kenosis* or "self-emptying." It began with God emptying his spirit, the *ruach Adonai*, into the nostrils of the first Adam; it ended with the sacrifice of the Second Adam on the cross, saying, "Into thy hands I commend my spirit." The Godhead is eternal life because it is always letting go of itself and throwing itself away. *Kenosis* is God eternally losing himself, and finding again by losing again—the cure of like by like, of Phosphorus vanquished by the Morning Star, of the Tree which brought death overcome by the death on the Tree.

The man who has died to his old identity finds, however, that not only his own past life, but also the lives of all other beings, are marvelously transfigured. What before seemed to be suffering and evil is now seen to be the playful hide-and-seek of God. From the viewpoint of conventional religion this is outrageous folly, as is likewise the attitude of living without anxiety for the future. There is, indeed, some analogy between the holy man and the crazy man, since both may be said to be "out of their minds," as having "lost themselves," or as being "thoughtless" or "care-less." In Russian Orthodoxy such a man is sometimes known as *Krista-rady yurodivy* or "fool for the sake of Christ."

> The *yurodivy* sees godliness and spirit shining out from all that is lowliest and "worst"; from the dust of the highway, the sharp stones that cut his feet, the thorns that tear his flesh, the biting winter frost, the intolerable heat of summer, the stench of the doss house; from the most degraded types of men and women. (16)

Or, as a modern Russian mystic puts it:

> Everybody can, at any time and in any place, see the Face of our Lord. Men of today are realistically minded, and, when the saints and the mystics come and tell them: "We have seen the Lord," they answer with Thomas: "Except I shall . . . thrust my hand into his side, I will not believe." Jesus accepts this challenge. He allows himself to be seen, and touched, and spoken to. Jesus shows us the poor, and the sick, and the sinners, and generally all men,

and tells us: "Behold my hands and my feet. . . .
Handle me and see; for a spirit hath not flesh and
bones, as ye see me have." (17)

This vision, this divine folly, this death of the old
identity does not come from daring. (My independent ego is the daring thing.) The vision comes from
seeing that there really is no other alternative, no
other way to go. . . . Here am I with Isaiah in the
temple, and I see "the Lord sitting upon a throne,
high and lifted up" and surrounded with the blazing
wings of seraphim, and I am scared out of my wits.
The space enlarges until I think that those wings are
each a thousand miles long, with colossal feathers of
living brass, and I am a little thing far down on the
downest floor. And the voice of the Most High, thun-
dering like "the sound of many waters," says, "As the
heavens are higher than the earth, so are my ways
higher than your ways, and my thoughts than your
thoughts." What on earth am I to do with someone
who can stage such a scene as this? I have to say,
"Yes, Lord! Yes, Lord! Just as you say, Lord! Oh, yes,
Lord; you are my Father, my support, and my maker,
and I just don't have a leg to stand on!"

Then, joined to the voice of the Lord, I hear the
voices of the Patriarchs and Prophets, Apostles and
Martyrs, Popes and Archbishops, Confessors and
Doctors, weighty with the authority and wisdom of
two thousand years, telling me that there is no common ground between God and myself; that he is Being and I am nothing; that he is the all-loving and the
all-righteous, and that I am just a contemptible little
jerk who doesn't even deserve the privilege of frying
in hell. By now, though flat on my face, I wish like

anything that I could get one look at those Eyes. If only I had the rubber necks of the people in the hymn who aspire

Prostrate before thy Throne to lie,
And gaze and gave on thee!

At the same instant I become aware of those Eyes watching me right through the back of my head— Eyes that bore implacably into the most tender and disreputable centers of my soul, that soon appear to surround me in all directions, to watch from the outside and from the inside, until everything is just One Eye. And because there is no brow, no face, I cannot tell what expression that Eye has. It just looks, and I can't stand it. I start running, running in blind panic down the corridors of the temple; but every way I turn I am running straight into that Eye. I drop to the floor, curl up, shut my eyes, and cover my head. Yet the Eye comes at me from deep inside me— vaster than ever, filling all thinkable space.

There is nowhere—nowhere at all—left to go. There isn't an inch for me to stand upon or to hide in; the only shred of myself that I can find is just the terror, the running away from that Eye. There remains nothing whatever to be done except for that Eye to look. There is nowhere for terror to go, no one to answer the screams, no darkness to cover me, no place to bury the body. And, just then, I am the Eye. For "the eye with which I see God," said Eckhart, "is the same eye with which God sees me."

VI

This Is My Body

To those nurtured in the culture of Europe and the Mediterranean, bread and wine are among the most beautiful gifts of life. I am thinking of *real* bread, not the edible foam-rubber of America. Real bread that is good to eat without butter, or even cheese; bread that still has flavor when dry. When I break open such a loaf there is just the faintest whiff of an old wooden flour mill, reflected in a weir-pond of the River Stour in Kent and standing before a tall cluster of beech trees. The harsh sighing of crows through the hot afternoon, and moss on the stone wall along the water. It is even more so with wine—this mystery of evocation, this magic of being able to bottle memories, and to ferment an essence of sun, and hills, and quiet villages, and the lazy days of late summer.

Some years ago I was the dean of an experimental graduate school where our faculty and students came from many different countries, and where the dominating interest was the study of comparative religions. I had made it a custom that, for those who wanted it, wine should always be served with dinner. (Tea and coffee, milk and water were also available.) It was never pressed upon anyone, but, to my astonishment, I learned that the custom had become a source of scandal—that it was a cause of raised eyebrows among Muslims and Hindus, and, even more so, among the Methodist-minded members of our university faculty. I was therefore strongly urged by some of my colleagues to discontinue the custom. "After all," they said, "it is really a trivial matter whether we have wine or not, and the reputation of the school is much more important."

Whereupon all my European and ancestral Christian hackles were raised, and I said, "Gentlemen, this is *not* a trivial matter. We are not living in Asia and eating Peking duck, or *tempura*, or *fagadu*, or *khichri*. We are in the West, eating the food of the West, and no person of true culture in the West takes his food without wine. As an institution of learning and culture, we are honor-bound to uphold the highest standards of our civilization!"

But my colleagues and spiritually minded critics were not convinced, for they could not understand anyone feeling so strongly about a "merely material" matter of food and drink. I soon began to realize that in the American bourgeoisie there is, contrary to general belief, a powerful trend of anti-material-ism amounting almost to a hatred of matter. For surely a materialist is a person who loves material— wood and leather, flax and silk, eggs and fruit, stone and glass, fish and bread, olives and wine. Yet, almost without exception, every American town and village looks as if it were made by people who loathed material, and wanted to convert it as fast as possible into heaps of rubbish. (This goes, also, for the industrial towns and "subtopias" of Europe and the New Asia.) Most of them are two walls of neon-lit "fronts" facing the highway, and backed with a shambles of shacks and wrecked cars. Even the nice residences of the north end of town are somehow scrubbed clean of life, as if it were a poisonous fungus. The kitchens look like operating rooms and everything that comes out of them tastes as if it had been washed in soap, and made by chemists instead of cooks.

The cooking of a culture is the real test of its attitude to the material universe, and by this test the Chinese and the French are exemplary materialists. The folk-cooking of America ranks, beyond doubt, with the worst in the world. Its values are purely quantitative, and it is eaten out of a sense of dietetic duty rather than love. Now that everything can be precooked, and then frozen, and then warmed over for serving, it is incomparably worse than ever before—worse than when Henry Miller wrote his essay on "The Staff of Life," which is the definitive critique of American cooking and one of the best belly-laughs in modern literature.

All jesting aside, however, I would point to such

cooking as the main sign that American culture is not only post-Christian but anti-Christian. Proper cooking can be done only in the spirit of a sacrament and a ritual. It is an act of worship and thanksgiving, a celebration of the glory of life, and no one can cook well who does not love and respect the raw materials he handles: the eggs and onions, the herbs and salts, the mushrooms and beans, and, above all, the living animals—fish, fowl, and flesh—whose lives we take to live. Ritual is not just a symbolism of formal gestures. Ritual is, basically, anything done with loving awareness and reverence—whether cooking, carpentry, fishing, writing a letter, performing surgery, or making love. The everyday life of the modern West is quite startlingly lacking in ritual, as in all the style and color that goes with it.

Now the central mystery, the chief act of Christian worship, is a matter of food and drink, the taking of bread and wine in communion as the flesh and the blood of Christ. By and large, the rite is now deplorably perfunctory. In the Catholic Church itself the bread looks, and tastes, like a plastic medal, and the wine isn't passed around. They are afraid someone may offend Jesus by spilling it. But even this is better than serving grape juice, like the Methodists.

The fact that the Eucharist (= Thanksgiving) of Bread and Wine is the central rite of Christianity represents the most important insight which Christianity (thanks in some measure to Judaism) has to offer to the sum of wisdom. This is something often missed by the Hindus and the Buddhists, and Christians themselves have only half-heartedly appreciated it. William Temple expressed it by saying that Christianity is the only truly materialist religion, the only religion (though Judaism and Islam must be included) which asserts unequivocally the goodness and glory of the physical universe, and believes that its creation was not a divine mistake. The Hindus and Buddhists are ambivalent here, for there is a strong tendency to feel that the *maya* of the world is to be transcended rather than loved. A minority of Hindu and Buddhist schools take an opposite view. But the Christian point of view is supposed to be that the Lord thoroughly delights in his *maya*, and that the heavens really do "declare the glory of God."

The meaning of the Eucharist is based on the fact that, in Mediterranean cultures at the time of Jesus, bread and wine were the staple food and drink. Bread was apparently the main item of food, with meat, vegetables and fruit used for a garnishing. In those times, wine came from the vineyards in a somewhat thicker consistency than now, and, before being passed to the individual cups, it was mixed with water in a large flat bowl or *crater*. (Hence the the continued custom of mixing water with the wine at Mass.) As the staple food and drink, bread and wine therefore constituted the material life of mankind, the physical body and blood, in that "man is what he eats."

Bread and wine are also sacrificial; there is no bread without the grinding of wheat and no wine without the crushing of grapes. This is the scandal of biological existence, that I cannot live without killing other creatures. So long as it is firmly felt that I am myself alone, and that the creatures of the plant and animal worlds are quite *other* than I, destroying them to feed myself cannot be done without guilt. This is so strongly sensed by the Hindus and Buddhists that they try to overcome the guilt of living-through-eating by *ahimsa*, the practice of maximal harmlessness by refraining from the destruction of all the higher forms of life, whether insect or bird, fish, reptile, or mammal. Yet this does not finally come to grips with the problem. Life still agonizes for us in the vegetable world.

Bread and wine are brought to the Mass not only as the gifts of nature—that is, as flour and grape juice. Our physical existence as men is also *our* work, and thus the flour is baked and the grape juice fermented. In short, the bread and wine offered at the altar for Mass (brought, in ancient times, by the people themselves) represent ourselves, our flesh and blood, and the work, the sacrifice, and the guilt which they involve.

The crux of the rite is that the bread and wine, which are ourselves, be transformed into the Body and Blood of Christ and then consumed by us. Could there be a more striking way of celebrating the union of Christ and mankind, God and universe? "Nothing else," said St. Leo, "is aimed at in our partaking of the Body and Blood of Christ than that we change into what we consume."

But there is more to it than that. For Jesus' hearers, the idea of eating his flesh and drinking his blood, even metaphorically, was quite startling.

"I am the bread of life. Your [fore]fathers ate manna in the wilderness and are dead. [But] this is the bread which comes down from heaven, that whoever eats of it should not die. I am that living bread come down from heaven. If anyone eats this bread, he shall live to eternity. For the bread which I shall give is my flesh, [given] for the life of the world."

The Jews began to argue with one another, saying, "How can this man give us [his] flesh to eat?"

Jesus said to them, "I *mean* this: unless you eat the flesh of the Son of Man, and drink his blood, you do not have life in yourselves. The eater of my flesh and the drinker of my blood has eternal life, and I will raise him up in the last day. For my flesh is true food and my blood is true drink. The eater of my flesh and the drinker of my blood abides in me, and I in him. Even as the living Father has sent me, and as I live through the Father, so he that eats me, he shall live through me. *This* is the bread which has come down from heaven—not such as your [fore]fathers ate, and then died. The eater of *this* bread shall live to eternity." . . .

Hearing this, many of his disciples said, "This is a rough saying; who can understand it?" . . .

From then, many of his disciples withdrew, and no longer went with him. (*John* 6: 48–58, 60, 66.)

Remember that one of the main prohibitions of the Jewish law was the drinking of blood. Blood was felt to be the life-essence of men and animals, and thus the property of God alone, so that every animal killed for food had to have its throat slit and the blood poured upon the ground. Therefore these words were as shocking to Jesus' listeners as if he had commanded incest. For the implication is that if only God may drink blood, to drink blood—and especially the blood of the Son of Man—is to have equality with God, and for that reason eternal life.

The Last Supper—the archetype of the Mass—was held under circumstances which had complex symbolical implications. It is clear from all four Gospels that Jesus went out of his way to challenge the Jewish "establishment," in full knowledge that this would bring the death penalty. He therefore brought the situation to a crisis at the time of the Passover, the feast whereby the Jews have always celebrated their deliverance from slavery in Egypt. Central to the Passover rite was the sacrifice of a lamb, at 3:00 P.M. on the Parasceve—that is, the day of preparation for the Sabbath (Saturday) upon which the Passover was held. This sacrifice repeated the original Passover sacrifice of the lamb whose blood was smeared upon the doorposts of the captive Hebrews to ward off the Lord's Destroying Angel, who, in that same night, killed all the first-born sons of the Egyptians. This is the origin of the "saving-Blood-of-the-Lamb" symbolism.

Jesus seems to have timed his own death to occur on the Parasceve (Friday), and to coincide with the sacrifice of the Passover lamb.[1] He was putting himself in place of the original lamb, to inaugurate a New Covenant (Testament, Dispensation, or Relationship) between God and man, a covenant that would give a new and vaster dimension of meaning to the old Passover symbolism of deliverance from Egypt. In this new dimension, captivity in Egypt no longer stood merely for the political defeats of the Jewish nation, nor the Passover for political liberation. "My kingdom," said Jesus, "is not of this world."

---

[1] The Synoptic Gospels—*Matthew, Mark,* and *Luke*—imply that the Last Supper was the Passover feast, but most modern scholars agree that the account in *John* has greater chronological accuracy, and that the Supper was therefore held on the Thursday before the Parasceve.

Captivity in Egypt now stood for the whole fallen state of mankind, and the New Passover for liberation from death, which the Fall had brought about. There is also the standpoint from which this is *still* a parabolic symbolism, from which "Egypt" is the Lord's *maya* or *kenosis* or self-forgetting, and "Passover" his awakening.[2]

The New Covenant has reference not only to the deliverance from Egypt, and the subsequent entry of the Hebrews into the Promised Land; it also refers back to the covenant made between the Lord God and Noah after the Flood.

> And God blessed Noah and his sons, and said unto them, "Be fruitful, and multiply, and replenish the earth. And the fear of you and the dread of you shall be upon every beast of the earth, and upon every fowl of the air, upon all that moveth upon the earth, and upon all the fishes of the sea; into your hand are they delivered. Every moving thing that liveth shall be meat for you; even as the green herb have I given you all things. But flesh with the life thereof, [which is] the blood thereof, shall yet not eat." (*Genesis* 9: 1–4. AV.)

And the commandment is repeated in *Deuteronomy:*

> Thou mayest eat flesh, whatsoever thy soul lusteth after. . . . Even as the roebuck and the hart is eaten, so thou shalt eat them: the unclean and the

[2] In this interpretation, the crossing of the Red Sea aligns itself with an almost universal symbolism of the Active Door—the Symplegades, the Strait Gate, the Needle's Eye, the Sword of Flame which "turns every way," and all those images of snapping jaws and whirling knives through which the hero must leap "in a moment, in the twinkling of an eye," if he is to find his way into heaven. It is the old story of "he who hesitates is lost," hesitation in this context being even the most momentary doubt of one's own eternity. (18)

clean shall eat of them alike. Only be sure that thou eat not the blood: for the blood is the life; and thou mayest not eat the life with the flesh. Thou shalt not eat it; thou shalt pour it upon the earth as water. . . . And thou shalt offer thy burnt offerings, the flesh and the blood, upon the altar of the Lord thy God: and the blood of thy sacrifices shall be poured out upon the altar of the Lord thy God, and thou shalt eat the flesh. (*Deuteronomy* 12: 20b, 22–24, 27. AV.)

Under the Old Covenant, the sacrifice is a communion, a common meal, between God and his people in which they take the flesh and he takes the blood.[8] But under the New Covenant, instituted by Jesus, the people are to have both the flesh and the blood of the sacrificial lamb. This is the condition of eternal —that is, *divine*—life, for God alone is eternal. There is no way to inherit eternal life except to be one with

---

[8] See the account in *Exodus* 24: 4–8 of the ritual sealing of the covenant after the delivery of the Law to Moses. The blood of the sacrificial animals is divided into two parts, of which one is poured out on the altar and the other sprinkled over the people. The learned biblical scholars Oesterley and Robinson have the following comment: "The meaning of this ritual is not far to seek. The blood is the life, the vital essence. Two parties, at present independent one of another, are to be united in a single whole, and, to secure the desired union, a third party is introduced. Its life is taken from it and made available for the other two. Both come under it, both are included in it, the same vital essence now covers and embraces the two. They are thus no longer independent entities, they are one, finding their unity with each other in their union with that third party whose blood now covers them both. Till this point is reached, however near they might have been brought to one another, they are merely contiguous; now they are continuous, and form parts of a single indivisible whole. We might almost say that Yahweh is Himself included in the term Israel; henceforward it will connote not merely a human community, but one of which He is a member." (19)

God, and, symbolically, this is to drink the blood as well as to eat the flesh.

> As they were eating, Jesus took bread, and blessed it, and broke it, and gave it to the disciples, and said, "Take, eat; this is my body." And he took the cup, and gave thanks, and gave it to them, saying, "All of you, drink from this; for this is my blood of the covenant, which is shed for many for the remission of sins." (*Matthew* 26: 26–28.)

St. Luke and St. Paul, in their accounts of the Supper, add the injunction, "Do this in remembrance of me." One wonders whether, through observing this commandment, the following generations of Christians have nurtured more love or more hatred amongst themselves. For was the "remembrance" simply a reminder, or was it the "representation," the making present again, of the veritable flesh and blood of the Son of God? And was that real presence spiritual, or was it sacramental—an actual conversion of the "substance" of bread and wine into Jesus himself? Today it seems incredible that men killed and tortured each other over such questions, or provoked so brutal a holocaust as the Thirty Years' War.

One reason was simply that they never understood the full significance of "remembrance" (in Greek, *anamnesis*). For to remember, especially in such a context as this, is not merely to call to mind an event that is past, nor merely to recall by naming (in the sense of the Aramaic *dukrana*). To remember is also to "re-collect," to gather together what has been scattered or divided. Likewise, to know or realize the truth is also to remember, for in Greek *alethes*

(= truth) is the "non-lethal"—what is recovered from the River Lethe, where the dead forget their past. This thought was continued into the Christian tradition. At the breaking of the bread in the Eastern Orthodox Mass, the priest says, "Broken and divided is the Lamb of God; broken, yet not disunited; ever eaten, yet never consumed, but sanctifying partakers." So also the *Didache* (first century) gives a eucharistic prayer with the image of the bread as the gathering together in unity of the wheat that was scattered upon the hills. Thus "in remembrance of me" is in recollection of the unity which exists before the apparent scattering or breaking of the One into the Many, before the entrancement of the Lord in his *maya*.

What does all this come to but the proclamation that man and the universe are an outpouring of love? The very being of each creature is God abandoning himself, for love is no other than *kenosis,* and the Sacrifice of the Lamb "slain from the foundation of the world" is no other than the slaying of all the living creatures by which living creatures live. Jesus is saying, in the symbolism of the Supper, that all flesh which is eaten is his flesh, and all blood which is shed is his blood. Do not, therefore, feel guilt for it any more. It is "shed for many for the remission of sins," remitted in the realization that all the wheat ground and the grapes crushed for us, all the steaks broiled and the fish grilled for us, are—along with the human corpses offered for worms and vultures— the innumerable disguises in which the Lord gives himself away.

That the Church has not absorbed this insight is

at once apparent from the form in which the Mass is celebrated in East and West alike. In the East, the bread and wine have been consecrated in a sanctuary closed off from the congregation by the icon screen. In the West, the altar was removed to the east end of the church and raised high upon steps, and Mass celebrated by the priest facing east and away from the people. (However, in recent years many Catholic churches have returned it to the central position.) This removal of the Sacrament to an enclosed or exalted position, together with the royal honors done to its presence, shows only that it was not assimilated. Practically speaking, Christ was treated as the juxtaposition instead of the union of the divine and the human. The mood of the Church toward the Sacrament has thus been that of the marvelous hymn in the Liturgy of St. James, *Sigisato pasa sarx*:

> Let all mortal flesh keep silence,
>   and with fear and trembling stand;
> Ponder nothing earthly-minded,
>   for with blessing in his hand
> Christ our God to earth descendeth,
>   our full homage to demand.
>
> Rank on rank the host of heaven
>   spreads its vanguard on the way,
> As the Light of Light descendeth
>   from the realms of endless day,
> That the powers of hell may vanish
>   as the darkness clears away.

The moment of Consecration comes with the warning of bells and a gathering of lights, and after the *Sanctus*—the adoration hymn of the angels—the priest's voice fades to an awed whisper. For the words "This is my Body" and "This is my Blood" will change bread and wine into the King of the Universe. In the mind's eye of the congregation, the Elements upon the altar become a center of light so intense that eyes must be lowered and thoughts put in order against its all-penetrating clarity. This is magnificent, but it is not yet the point. These are people who have decided to have their cake instead of eating it, for there is the reverent comfort of having one's God in a safe and sure place. In the form of the Host, the sacred Bread, he can be sealed away in the mysterious shrine of the tabernacle, and honored with ever-burning lights—which is why Catholic churches have an atmosphere of *presence* hardly found elsewhere. On solemn occasions he can be displayed for adoration in the golden sunburst of the monstrance, and even carried in the streets in jubilant procession, as at the feast of Corpus Christi, when little girls scatter rose petals before his path.

The danger of having one's cake instead of eating it is that it may go bad. It was a going bad, a mixed accumulation of superstition and mechanical piety, which provoked the Protestant revolution against the Mass and against altar-centered Christianity. But here, if ever, was a case of throwing out the Baby with the bath water. Or, to mix our metaphors a little, in a misguided enthusiasm for destroying idols, the Protestants threw away the egg instead of just breaking the shell.

But the positive contribution of the Reformation was its renewal of the *impossibility* of Christianity, by an increase of stress on moral endeavor. In the generally sunny atmosphere of Catholicism, the love of God is handed out rather too freely; the Sacrament of Penance gets rid of guilt for a couple of Hail Marys (so why bother with your analyst?), and its pervasively festive feeling all too easily encourages dancing at night in the plaza and being much too familiar with Rosa and Geneviève, Maria and Conchita. Although Luther insisted that salvation was by faith alone (not works), and Calvin by predestination alone, the theological theory—as is quite usual—had nothing to do with the practice. All through its history the effectual stress of Protestantism has been upon works—not the symbolic works of piety, but the practical works of industry and frugality, and the development of strong inhibitions against lust and luxury. And, after the middle of the nineteenth century, Protestants began seriously to acquire a social conscience.

Catholicism and Protestantism work in a curious alliance to intensify the individual's sense of separation from God. The former brings the divine into the closest physical proximity through the sacraments, and yet holds it off by the very intensity of adoration.[4] The latter aggravates the sense of individual responsibility, inculcates a permanent sense of guilt as a form of virtue, and, by esthetic mortifica-

---

[4] The Sacrament of Penance (i.e., "Confession") which so easily and kindly absolves one of sin and guilt, nevertheless most subtly reimposes the bond from which it has given freedom. For the true effectiveness of absolution depends upon the penitent's sincere resolve to amend his way of life. The form of confession requires him to say, "For these and all my other sins which I cannot now remember, I am heartily sorry, firmly purpose amendment, and humbly ask pardon of God," etc. But to say these things at all raises doubt as to whether one really means them.

tion, fosters a unique atmosphere of spiritual gloom. (I am not speaking of modern "liberal Protestantism," but of that "old-time Bible religion.")

Yet this intensification of the sense of separation, of one's own guilt and of God's transcendent otherness, of one's own nothingness and of God's regal glory, is simply building up pressure behind that very dam or block between the human and the divine which must be broken down. And there is no way to hasten its collapse like building up the pressure, bringing the sense of sin and separateness to a festering head, as with a boil.

From this point of view, then, one must encourage and applaud the characteristic attitudes of Catholicism and Protestantism, rejoicing in the fact that the further they are pressed, the nearer is a splendid liberation. From this point of view, an entirely new light is shed upon the most thorny features of Christianity—hair shirts and kneeling upon chains, bloody crucifixes and skulls, permanently enclosed nuns and ever-silent Trappists, Ignatian meditations on everlasting damnation and Presbyterian sermons on divine wrath, the refinements of Spanish prudery and the Bible-and-birchrod education of Fundamentalist children, the jeweled and brocaded splendor of Solemn Mass at St. Peter's and the dark-brown, varnished pitch-pine Gothic of the First Baptist Church with that ineffably abominable yellow glass. Looked at in the perspective of the Lord's eternal dance of hide-and-seek, these are the writhings which precede revelation; they are like the pangs of a woman in labor, but here in labor for the birth of a new kind of consciousness and a new apprehension of man's identity.

It is in this sense that Christianity is, to appropriate Karl Barth's phrase, a theology of crisis. But this particular crisis has two dangers. One is that it can fizzle out into mere secularism. People can simply have enough of the pressure, and give up. To hell with it; let's just live! The other is that one can get stuck in crisis for its own sake, not realizing that it should lead to something beyond itself. This is the danger of modern Christian obscurantism, whether it be the grim Jansenism of Irish-American Catholicism, or the sophisticated Bible-banging of Protestant Neo-orthodoxy.[5] In both cases, the danger arises from the stubborn conceit of spiritual exclusivism which the Church (and also Hitler's National Socialism) seems to have inherited from post-Exilic Judaism, with its fanatical insistence on racial purity and

---

[5] Jansenism, named after Bishop Cornelius Jansen, was a French Catholic movement of the early seventeenth century, somewhat akin in spirit to Calvinism, and based on a revival of St. Augustine's theology with its bias toward the theory of salvation through predestination rather than free will. As is usually the case, Jansen's reasonably moderate position was exaggerated by his followers, and Jansenism followed the paradoxical pattern of Calvinism. That is to say, the original emphasis on man's total dependence upon God's grace does a reverse flip into an emphasis upon rigorous discipline and purism. For many years Irish priests were trained in Jansenist institutions on the Continent, and for this reason Irish and, subsequently, American Catholicism has a strong puritanical flavor. Protestant Neo-Orthodoxy is especially associated with the work of Karl Barth, Emil Brunner, Reinhold Niebuhr, Hendrik Kraemer and others—all theologians of this century, stressing the unique and authoritative revelation of God in the Bible, though in a far more scholarly and sophisticated manner than the old-fashioned Fundamentalists.

exclusive election to divine favor. It is characteristic of these inheritors of Ezra and Nehemiah, whether Christian or Islamic, that they are perfectly assured of possessing the supreme revelation of God, before even deigning to examine any other spiritual tradition. This seriously curtails the number of theologians capable of looking at Christianity within the context of less exclusive views of the universe. There is, then, no real working out of a metatheology, and thus no framework in terms of which Christianity can find a resolution for its own perpetual state of crisis, no midwife for its now overprolonged pains of labor.

I say "overprolonged" because the Christian personality lives now in a vastly expanded world, culturally and technologically, where this special sense of identity and of exclusive spiritual privilege cannot be maintained without suicidal violence involving both other peoples and the natural environment. The question is whether the mythos of the Incarnation, of Godmanhood, of the life-giving Sacrifice of the Lord's Body and Blood, and of the incorporation of the world in the Mystical Body has any further relevance for this expanded and dangerously explosive civilization. Its principal relevance is, of course, that it has largely created the crisis, both by the force of direct inspiration and by the force of the rationalist-secularist revolution *against* the Church. The philosophy of any tyranny determines the philosophy of the rebellion!

In retrospect we can see that the Reformation intensified the Christian crisis without resolving it. We can see also that the same is true of Western rationalism and humanism, since they issue in a sense of man's identity and of his alienation from nature which is an exaggeration of the Christian ego. There follows, then, the irresistible question: Is it not possible that Christians might accept and assimilate the full implications of the Incarnation and of membership in the Body of Christ? That they should discover what it must finally mean to eat the Lord's Body and to drink his Blood? This does not mean that "Christianity" becomes absorbed into some kind of "Hinduism"—although, must we really make so much fuss about the label on the bottle? The point is rather that the "Hindu" myth of the Lord's *maya,* and of all beings as existing by his *atma-yajna* or self-sacrifice, not only gives the Christian myth a new and peculiar profundity; it acts as a catalyst through which there can be a full expression of Christian materialism. Or, if that sounds too partisan, let us call it a way of life in which what have hitherto been known as the spiritual and the material are brought into one.

For there has not yet existed a religion or a philosophy in which there is a true marriage of Heaven and Earth. There have been many approximations, but never one in which each said to the other, without any shadow of reservation, "I love you with all my heart!" We have seen the spiritual reduced to the material, and the material vaporized in the spiritual. We have seen unhappy compromises in which the spiritual is always saying to the material, "Yes, *but* . . ." We have seen the material perpetually damned with faint praise and always being talked down for the odd reason that it constantly changes and flows away, as if that were something wrong. Only most occasionally have Hindus had the courage to swing fully with the Lord in dancing his *maya,* and to stop insinuating that in some nasty, niggling last analysis the physical universe shouldn't be happening. Christian theologians, too, seem to have a commission to *protect* the Deity from full union with his universe, as if this would somehow completely subvert his morals. Indeed, they allow that the creature may participate in, reflect, be adopted into, transfigured by, or given unity with his Creator. But always, at the end of the line, there is someone wagging his finger and saying, *"But . . .* never forget, little creature, that you are nothing, nothing right down to your miserable essence, for your being is not your own." So—my body is God's, my mind is God's, my being itself is God's, all on loan to nothing and no one.

But if I'm not here, I know Who is!

The basic difficulty seems to be that people in religious circles always need someone or something to blame. I even catch myself doing it when I think about Baptist preachers. Religion somehow attracts those who like to lay down the law and point the finger of accusation, seldom realizing, incidentally, that the congregation just adores a colorful scolding. So I would like to say this without condemning anyone, preachers included. The thing is to see all faces as the masks of God, all characters as his roles, preachers included. Toward the end of his life that extraordinary Hindu-Buddhist-Muslim saint, the poet Kabir, used to look around and ask, "To whom shall I preach?" He saw the face and the activity of his Beloved in every direction.

Obviously, as so many Christians seem to fear, this vision of God-as-all might be used as a rationalization for indulgence in total wickedness. But fire is not untrue, or something to be abolished, because it can be used to burn people alive. What they really seem to fear is that, if God is all in all, the wicked will not get their just deserts; someone may lose the satisfaction of knowing that evildoers are going to be boiled in oil and devoured by spiders forever and ever. At this point it becomes more and more difficult to separate the wicked from the moralists who want to see them properly judged.

In a larger perspective these theological objections are trivial. They are like avoiding broiled salmon for fear of the bones, or living for fear of dying. It is all a colossal haggling and footling over technicalities, a metaphysical filibuster subconsciously designed to postpone the great moment of awakening. Perhaps it is like a woman being interminably difficult to woo, so as to build up all that more passion for the moment when she finally yields. Enough, however, is enough. The moment has arrived when a really thoroughgoing spiritual materialism is the intelligent and essential attitude for the management of technology, and for helping mankind to be something better than the most predatory monster yet evolved.

In fact, it is impossible to be a true materialist without being a mystic as well. The would-be materialist who renounces mysticism is either a slob or a bore. Or both, for there is something profoundly dreary about mere sensuality—the unrelieved panorama of filet mignon, bosoms and bottoms, Châteauneuf-du-Pape, Alfa Romeos and Chris-Crafts, dry martinis, scrolls by Sesshu, Pro Musica on hi-fi, Chanel No. 5, and even, alas, water, clouds, light, sand, and mountains beyond. After a while the bottoms feel like plastic. Still more dreary is the *sensible* materialism of the practical and provident, who will scrounge all their lives to provide themselves with leisure when they can no longer enjoy it. Or the academic materialist who is, perhaps, a scientific empiricist or a logical positivist or a "sound" statistical psychologist, whose real aim is to demonstrate that all nature is perfectly banal and dull. The trouble with this fellow is that no one ever mixed raven's blood with his mother's milk. He is marvelously and uncannily bereft of any sense that existence is odd.

At the other extreme, the pure mystic is like pure alcohol, or like a wine without body. Intense, strongly principled, quiet-mannered and unobtrusive, devastatingly simple in his needs and colorless in his tastes—no belly-laugh, no good roll with a girl in the hay, no gentle grin of understanding as between man and man—this one, with his terrifying sincerity, is more of a Euclidean proposition than a human being. Spirituality needs a beer and a loud burp, just as sensuality needs a bed on the hard ground, a rough blanket, and a long look at the utterly improbable stars.

The difficulty with the material world is that it collapses when you lean on it and turns to a fine powder when you clutch it. Material pleasure, even of the most refined order, is never enough, if "enough" is what you are seeking. If there is that strange, deep longing in the heart for something that is "the answer"—the gorgeous, golden glory you have always wanted but have never been able to find or define, the thing that is finally for real and for keeps, the eternal home—then anything in the physical or intellectual universe that is asked to be *that* will collapse. But it is sour grapes to despise the material world for that reason.

The answer, the eternal home, will never, never be found so long as you are seeking it, for the simple reason that it is yourself—not the self that you are aware of and that you can love or hate, but the one that always vanishes when you look for it. As soon as you realize that you *are* the Center, you have no further need to see it, to try to make it an object or an experience. This is why the mystics call the highest knowledge unknowing.

> That which is not seen by the eye, but by which the eyes see; *that*, understand truly, is Brahman and not what the world worships. (20)

When the material world is no longer asked to provide the eternal home it is suddenly and amazingly transfigured. Its impermanence becomes a dance instead of a mockery—and when it no longer mocks us there is no need to hate it, with hair shirts and flagellations on the one hand, or with bulldozers and barbarous cooking on the other.

The material world so seen is "the new heaven and the new earth" which, according to the *Apocalypse*, are to be created in the Last Day. It is likewise the body resurrected and the Paradise Garden. For death and the Last Day are when our conventional identity comes to the end of its tether and we "give up the ghost" of the isolated ego. We must not confuse the transfigured universe of eternity, the "life of the world to come," with the monstrous notion of a physical universe containing the risen bodies of all our friends and relations permanently pickled in Spirit. Innumerable accounts of this transfigured vision of the material world are to be found in the literature of mystical experience and paranormal states of consciousness, and it is surely through the transformation of consciousness rather than through the gate of literal death that we should expect to find the entrance to Heaven.

> The angels keep their ancient places;—
> Turn but a stone, and start a wing!
> 'Tis ye, 'tis your estrangèd faces,
> That miss the many-splendoured thing.

For there are sudden "slips" of consciousness into a wave length or dimension of this everyday world which impress those who see them as being more real than the normal vision. These "slips" are relatively common and must have been so throughout human history, and it seems to me unquestionable that they are the actual basis for doctrines of Paradise and of an ultimate transfiguration of the world. Thus, in a grimy railroad station:

> Suddenly, I was aware of some mysterious current of force, subtle, yet of unimagined potency, which seemed to sweep through that small drab waiting-room. A kind of glory descended upon the gathered company—or so it seemed to me. I looked at the faces of those around me and they seemed to be suffused with an inner radiance. I experienced in that moment a sense of profoundest kinship with

each and every person there. I loved them all!—but
with a kind of love I had never felt before. It was an
all-embracing emotion, which bound us together in-
dissolubly in a deep unity of being. I lost all sense
of personal identity then. These people were no
longer strangers to me. I *knew* them all. We were
no longer separate individuals, each enclosed in his
own private world, divided by all the barriers of social convention and personal exclusiveness. We were
one with each other and with the Life which we all
lived in common. (21)

In its earlier ages the Church was in constant ex-
pectation of the Parousia, the Second Coming of the
Lord, not in the obscurity of the manger but in the
full panoply of the King of Heaven, in the midst of
his angelic hosts. As the centuries have passed without Gabriel's trumpet rending the skies, this expecta-
tion has largely fizzled out, except in the lunatic
fringe of Protestantism. Obviously, the Church has
been looking for the Parousia in the wrong direction
—in the outward skies and not in the realm of heaven which is "within." The true Parousia comes at
the moment of crisis in consciousness, not in the
world of newspaper reality.

If anyone says to you, "Look, here is the Messiah", or, "There he is", do not believe it. Impostors
will come claiming to be messiahs or prophets, and
they will produce great signs and wonders to mis-
lead even God's chosen, if such a thing were possible. See, I have forewarned you. If they tell you,
"He is in the wilderness", do not go out; or if they
say, "He is there in the inner room", do not believe
it. Like lightning from the east, flashing as far as the
west, will be the coming of the Son of Man. (*Matthew* 24: 23–27. NEB.)

The great flash of lightning which, sensibly or meta-phorically, comes with these openings of conscious-ness is one of their most usual features.

It is possible, therefore, to envision a Church, a Christianity, in which Godmanhood is fully realized, in which the Incarnation has been assimilated, and which—in this everyday world—is already living beyond the Parousia in the glory of Heaven. This will not be a preaching Church, not a finger-wagging, Bible-banging, breast-thumping, floor-licking Church. It will be the Church of All Fools, laughing like Dante's angels. Laughing because it has just seen through the enormous trick that the Lord has played on himself in pretending to be us—scaring the Liv-ing Daylight out of himself by acting the lonely ego tormented by sin, with death and hell at last. Laugh-ing itself to tears because the whole world has been completely misunderstood: for it has been looked at with a spotlight called consciousness so narrow in scope that it was all but impossible to see how things are actually related. But only in that relationship do things have their meaning and their beauty, as well as their existence. *Ex divina pulchritudine esse om-nium derivatur.*

It may come to such a pass that churches, in the sense of buildings and ecclesiastical organizations, will fall into irrelevance—but only, I think, in that they will drop the conceit of being absolutely nec-essary, of being medicinally good for people. For ritual is really the same sort of expression as music, poetry, dancing, sculpture and painting, besides being an integrative art employing many other arts. Protestants and secularists are as starved for ritual as auto salesmen for poetry. These things are necessary, but only when done in the spirit of not being necessary. It is healthy to play, but you are not playing when you do it as a duty!

When I was a university chaplain I used to tell the students that they must *not* come to church out of a sense of duty. If that was why they came, we didn't want them, because they would be skeletons at the banquet. Worship, I told them, was making "celestial whoopee," and if they felt no urge to make it, it was better that they stayed in bed or went for a swim. I was speaking not of rousing gospel hymns and hearty handshakes at the door, but of pure glee in Solemn Mass with Gregorian chant.

The marvelously basic ritual of the Mass will doubtless remain. For centuries it has had the flavor of a court ceremonial, and, indeed, many of its particular ceremonies were derived from the courtly manners of Byzantium and Rome, and the ancient design of the church building is called *basilica*—the court of a king. All that is highly appropriate so long as we are down here and God is up there. At that stage both the cosmology and the worship of Christianity are *political*—a product of the culture of cities, projecting upon the cosmos the political concept of order-by-imposition from above.

But should not the imagery of membership in the Body of Christ, as of "I am the Vine and you are the branches," suggest a style of order that is not political but organic? [6] Whereas political order is main-

[6] See the much fuller discussion of this problem in my *Nature, Man and Woman*, Part I, Ch. I, "Urbanism and Paganism." Pantheon Books. New York, 1958.

tained by force from above, being *imposed*, organic order arises through the mutual and reciprocal interplay of forces within a field. Armies and machines are ordered politically. But human bodies, forests, ocean-floor communities, biological and botanical regions, planetary biospheres, and, probably, stellar galaxies are ordered organically.

In the Mass of the *basilica* the altar is the throne, and it puts Christ with his back to the wall like a monarch, flanked with his guards and fearful of attack from behind. In the Mass of the Body, or of the Vine, the altar is central, and the action of the Mass is not *oriented*, not facing eastward to some end out there, beyond, exalted, far in the future; the action is *radial*, for the kingdom is no longer above but within, no longer future but present. The Church is not, then, where the people come to court (and note how the Protestant church is modeled on the judicial instead of the monarchical court); the Church is where people come to celebrate the pattern of being One Body with Christ—not to kowtow, not to hear a catalogue of oughts and shoulds, but to make a ritual expression of the delight and splendor of Heaven and Earth in unity.

Some approximation to the radial Mass is now to be found in many Catholic churches under the influence of the so-called Liturgical Movement, based on the principle that the original meaning of liturgy, the act of worship, is a *leitos ourgos* or "work of the people"—a rite in which all present *participate* and not merely a sacerdotal drama *witnessed* by the people. Yet this is, alas, apt to go hand in hand with a rationalization, popularization and, thus, vulgarization of the liturgy in the superstition that the Mass ought to be "intelligible" in the literal, historical and theological-seminary sense of intelligibility. The Liturgical Movement therefore presses for Mass in the vernacular, and for the "dialogue Mass" in which the whole congregation joins in the responses.

But the Roman Catholic Church has no traditional feeling for Mass in the vernacular as compared, for example, with the Anglican and Greek Orthodox Churches. Translations into the vernacular are made by moralists instead of poets, and are then conducted in the prayer-wheel style, which, however magical and mantric in mumbled Latin, sound in English like the rituals of a stock exchange or tobacco auction. Latin is a veil of mystery which, when removed, reveals the Roman Liturgy in all the nakedness of its commercialized poverty.

The Church cannot celebrate a truly radial Mass without a shift in spiritual experience parallel to the shift in ritual. It is an empty gesture to move the altar to the center of the church without that changed sense of identity in which God is found to be the center of man. Otherwise, the altar at the center is still being treated as the altar at the East, where God is approached as an external and imperious power, an alien authority who judges and compels us from beyond and above. The radial Mass represents an entirely different order of creation, the hierarchy of the Vine and the branches, in which all terms of the "above," the "exalted," and the "high-and-mighty" are transposed into terms of what is deeply "within," "essential," and "ultimately real." Man and the universe become concentric with instead of eccentric to God.[7]

As I am not trying to write a liturgical manual, I will not attempt to dwell on the form of a radial Mass as it might ideally be celebrated. The traditional liturgies have rightly avoided dramatics, such as prayers recited with "feeling," in preference for a serenely impersonal style of utterance. The whole theory of the liturgy is that true worship is not man speaking to God, but God speaking through man. Worship is the action in which man is drawn into the vortex of love which revolves eternally between the Persons of the Trinity. In the Mass, the congregation becomes God the Son speaking to the Father with the words of the Spirit, and therefore the saying and singing of these words should forbid the intrusion of personal idiosyncrasies. This is why the Gregorian chant has been the most perfect vehicle for the Western liturgy, since it is entirely free of military bombast and personalized sentimentality. It is pre-eminently the music of contemplation, and of a majestic serenity that has no need for pomp. Yet even in its most triumphant moods it is profoundly and marvelously sad, because it is the music of God in exile, and thus of the human ego possessed with a longing which is as deep as it is undefined. The ever-recurring patterns of brain tissue supporting mem-

[7] Several American Catholic bishops have recently (1963) objected to the radial Mass on the grounds that when an army is on the march or a delegation presents a formal address to a superior, all members face in one direction. . . . In Tokyo novelty shops you can buy switch-blade knives disguised as crucifixes.

ories billions of years old. Gregorian chant is always touched with the metaphysical nostalgia of the *Salve Regina:*

> To thee we exiles, children of Eve, lift our crying. To thee we are sighing, as mournful and weeping, we pass through this vale of sorrow. . . . Hereafter, when our earthly exile shall be ended, show us Jesus, the blessed fruit of thy womb. O gentle, O tender, O gracious Virgin Mary.

I can only suppose, then, that in a truly post-exilic Church the Mass would indeed be a *celebration*. It would be—at last—an expression of being unashamedly glad to exist, of being a community without moral humbug and (therefore) mutual mistrust, and of knowing that, though our individual forms come and go like the waves, we are each and all the eternal ocean. As things are, we do not have the nerve to celebrate in this way without feeling vaguely guilty and ill at ease. Won't the gods be jealous of our happiness and take it as an affront? Won't it relax our guard against those powers of darkness which, as the hymn says, "prowl and prowl around" plotting our downfall?

As there is not yet a religion in which Heaven says to Earth, "I love you with all my heart," so there is not yet a ritual which embodies metaphysical *joie de vivre*. Now, there is a tendency in ritualism to be too symbolic. Ceremonies tend to represent or to memorialize or to prefigure something that actually takes place elsewhere. Marriage is not consummated at the altar, and at Holy Communion there is neither substantial eating or drinking nor expression of love between the participants. Some Early Christian literature suggests that at one time the Communion and the Agape (i.e., the "love feast" now moldered into the parish breakfast) were held at the same time, or were even the same event. But apparently things got out of hand: the drinking became drunkenness and the loving became too amorous.

For the problem is that when Heaven says to Earth, "I love you with all my heart," it follows that this love must include and accept the Earth's delight in sexuality. Thus there was apparently a tendency in the primitive Church for the eucharistic feast to "revert" to the ritual orgy in which men and women acted out, in community, the marriage of Heaven and Earth. But this was exactly the abominable Baal-cult of Canaan and the worship of Ishtar against which the Hebrew prophets had so fervently fulminated. This was, too, the very nadir of the spirit's entrapment in the sucking quicksand of the flesh from which both the Orphic and Neo-Platonic traditions of Greek wisdom sought deliverance. In Christianity these Hebrew and Greek associations of the orgiastic with the loathsome came together as Biblical myth and Greek philosophy coalesced into Christian theology. Therefore as a religion uniquely preoccupied with the negative fascination of sex, the last thing that the Church could tolerate would be any expression of physical love (be it polymorphous or genital) in its corporate worship.

Accordingly, the Mass has become the non-Communion of Saints—an exercise in which the participants appear dressed from neck to sole in the full panoply of their social role and status, to parade stiffly before the altar with eyes to the front and each in his own private devotional scene with the Lord. At best, the Church overwhelms this parade of masks with temples in which the worshipers become rustling and veiled shadows, individually and collectively lost in huge, dim spaces of stone—spaces where the rite is centered among the lights in the high distance, and the arches murmur and call to each other above the sanctuary, where priests and acolytes move as tiny figures beneath the vastness of heaven. The individual Christian can creep quietly into this scene, unnoticed by any but God, and feel himself lifted for a time into the transcendental world.

But he cannot *stay* there without becoming a churchmouse—or perhaps a clergyman, and pay for it by spending the rest of his life in black serge and starched linen. As a child in an English village, I remember the pious little ladies whose cottages huddled close to the parish church—the faithful core of the congregation, who attended Mass every morning and were constantly in and out of the church like the jackdaws in the belfry, in the attempt to stay as permanently as possible in the Lord's house. Moths around the fire of ecclesiastical magic, tantalized by vague glimpses of the Beatific Vision, flickering momentarily from highlights on the altar candlesticks and the golden chalice, but all demurely muffled in cassocks and surplices, the upholstery on the people instead of the furniture, and everyone meekly shepherded into stalls and pens and pews.

O how lovely are thy dwellings, thou Lord of hosts! My soul hath a desire and longing to enter into the

courts of the Lord; my heart and my flesh rejoice
in the living God.

Yea, the sparrow hath found her an house, and the
swallow a nest where she may lay her young:
even thy altars, O Lord of hosts, my King and my
God.

Blessed are they that dwell in thy house; they will
be always praising thee. . . .

For one day in thy courts is better than a thousand.

> (*Psalm* 84: 1–4, 10. BCP mod.)

Somehow the psalmist's aspiration for the rejoicing
of his flesh in the living God doesn't quite come off
in churchly circles. The Word becomes flesh, but
only as far down as the neck.

VII

The Sacred Taboo

Is it, then, possible to celebrate the union of Heaven and Earth in a religion which has consistently held that sexual love is disgusting? Not only disgusting, but profoundly sinful except between married couples for the sole purpose of reproduction.

One must be most careful of jumping to superficial conclusions in trying to understand Christian attitudes to sex. For there is a sense in which Christianity is *the* religion about sex, and in which sex plays a more important role even than in Priapism or Tantric Yoga. In any Christian milieu the subject of sex is extremely touchy; it is what embarrasses most easily, what is surrounded with the most rigid rules of conduct, and what arouses the most unintelligent emotions. This indicates not only a deep preoccupation with sex, but also the direction in which we must look for basic understanding of Christianity as a whole and of the mystery that lies at its heart.

On the surface, almost all forms of Christianity seem to be militantly prudish, even though, in quite recent times, there has arisen the practice of damning sexuality with faint praise. I was not merely joking when I said that, today, the churches function mainly as societies for regulating familial ties and sexual mores. There is a practical test. One has simply to ask: For what principal reason are people excommunicated, and priests or ministers defrocked? For pride, vainglory and hypocrisy? For envy, hatred, malice and all uncharitableness? For gluttony or sloth? For ownership of slums or of shares in shady loan companies? For coldness of heart or a cruel tongue? Not on your life. You can live openly in such sins and hold a bishopric.

But once it is discovered that you have an irregular marriage, that you consort with a mistress or a lover, that you take pleasure in unconventional modes of intercourse, or, worse, that you are actively homosexual, you are in real trouble. You must stop it at once or get out. The only other sin that seriously bothers the Church is open heresy, and then only in the more conservative denominations. This overwhelming preoccupation with the sins of sex is reflected in popular speech, where "immorality" almost always means sexual immorality, and "living in sin" means irregular cohabitation.

There have been times, and there still are places,

where the Church simply winks at sacerdotal concubinage and canon lawyers arrange easy annulments of marriage. But such attitudes usually go hand in hand with a general atmosphere of skepticism and cynicism, when the ecclesiastical authorities have lost interest in religion and are simply going through the motions. Generally speaking, where and whenever the Church takes itself seriously, there are no such concessions, and the zealous priest has beside him his manual of moral theology, arranged according to the Ten Commandments, wherein the discussion of "Thou shalt not commit adultery" occupies at least two thirds of the volume.

Many theologians recognize that this is a serious distortion of Christian ethics, pointing out that Jesus was lenient and compassionate toward those who had "sinned in the flesh," as contrasted with his rage against hypocrisy and exploitation of the poor. They also try to make a case for the idea that sex within the bonds of Holy Matrimony is a sacred and beautiful thing because it is no longer "depersonalized," no longer "cheapened" by being a pleasure taken with any congenial partner, but ennobled in becoming the seal of a life-long and total commitment to a single person.

For some reason these (quite modern) attempts to say a good word for erotic love sound curiously throttled and lacking in conviction. The reason is, of course, that they are plain humbug. A Christian may write poetry about mountains and quiet forests and all the "beauties of nature" as expressions of the beauty of nature's Lord. He may adorn the church and the altar with images of flowers and birds, fishes and stars. But what if the Christian poet should have something to say about the revelation of divine glory in the image of a naked girl, upon her marriage bed, squirming with bliss in the arms of her man? Imagine the screens and niches of St. Peter's adorned with Baroque equivalents of the tantric sculptures that embellish Hindu temples! Or what if the "young married" group should meet at the First Presbyterian on Wednesday evenings for the sacrament of "prayer through sex"?

Such expressions of piety are totally inconceivable within the present temper of Christendom. God may be seen and worshiped in nature just so long as sex is left out of it. Thus it is perfectly acceptable to sing:

> For the beauty of each hour
> Of the day and of the night,
> Hill and vale, and tree and flower,
> Sun and moon, and stars of light,
> Lord of all, to thee we raise
> This our hymn of grateful praise.

Yet what if the choir were to burst into an anthem as follows?

> How beautiful are thy feet with shoes, O prince's
> daughter! the joints of thy thighs are like jewels,
> the work of the hands of a cunning workman.
> Thy navel is like a round goblet, which wanteth not
> liquor: thy belly is like an heap of wheat set
> about with lilies.
> Thy two breasts are like young roes that are twins.
> Thy neck is as a tower of ivory;
> thine eyes like the fishpools in Heshbon, by the
> gate of Bath-rabbim:
> thy nose is as the tower of Lebanon which look-
> eth toward Damascus.

Thine head upon thee is like Carmel, and the hair
   of thine head like purple. . . .
How fair and how pleasant art thou, O love, for
   delights!
This thy stature is like to a palm tree,
   and thy breasts to clusters of grapes.
I said, "I will go up to the palm tree, I will take
   hold of the boughs thereof:
   now also thy breasts shall be as clusters of the
   vine,
   and the smell of thy nose like apples;
And the roof of thy mouth like the best wine for my
   beloved, that goeth down sweetly, causing the
   lips of those that are asleep to speak."

I know of no denomination of the Church in which
this song would be formally inadmissible, seeing that
it is taken from the Holy Scriptures themselves (*Song
of Songs* 7: 1–9, AV.), and the explanatory gloss in
my copy of the Bible says of this section, "The
Church professeth her faith in Christ," though I
think it should read, "Christ professeth his love for
the Church." Nevertheless, who would be so rash as
to take up the precedent?

But the very fact that sexual love and overt sexual
imagery is the principal Christian taboo points directly to what must be, in fact, the *mysterium tremendum*, the inner and esoteric core of the religion.
For whatever is taboo is not just something forbidden as an evil. Christianity forbids murder, but
stands in no awe of it, and there has never been any
censorship of the depiction and description of murder. Strictly speaking, a taboo is something to be
avoided because it is mighty and holy, something to
be handled with reverence because it is wonderful

and dangerous like fire. Sex is not to be described for the same reason that the Name of God, YHVH, is not to be uttered, and not to be depicted for the same reason that no graven image of God may be made. This is not to say that sexual intercourse is itself the heart of the matter. It is rather that this act of generation and love and self-abandonment is the supreme symbol of God, and may, under certain conditions, be a direct way of realizing the mystical union.

Yet how could this be true if the characteristic reaction of pious people to sexuality is not so much awe as disgust? Furthermore, even those great mystics who are supposed to represent whatever there may be of an esoteric aspect to Christianity seem, on the whole, to share this distaste. An obvious exception must be made of those few and extremely bold female mystics who suggest that the real reward for their virginity is to be intercourse with Jesus himself—for example, St. Margaret Mary Alacoque, who was the champion of the cult of the Sacred Heart. It is, however, quite obvious that sexual disgust is usually an emotion misnamed, for it is by no means the same disgust that one feels for sewage or rotting corpses. As psychopathologists have long known, sexual disgust is a "negative fascination." It is the sensation of lust as perceived by those who will not recognize it as such, and who interpret it as loathing because of the convulsive sensations common to both orgasm and nausea. Such misidentification carried out, as it were, behind the back of one's own mind makes it possible to enjoy the things of the Devil while taking the side of the Lord, and those who make much of their distaste for sex lose few opportunities for exercising it.[1]

The question has often been raised as to whether Christianity (and in particular Catholicism) has an esoteric aspect, since it seems almost incredible that the highly intelligent and cultured individuals whom one finds at the top of the Roman hierarchy can swallow the plain superstitions of the Catechism. Outsiders often wonder, therefore, whether such high ecclesiastics are just cynical purveyors of the "opiate of the people," following the philosophy of Dostoevsky's Grand Inquisitor to placate their conscience, or whether they are initiates to a higher interpretation of the crude dogmatic forms. It has even been suggested that the visible and official Pope in Rome is a Black or Shadow Pope who takes his orders from a White Pope completely unknown to the public, and that the latter presides over an inner Church with a secret discipline and doctrine.

Such notions are doubtless romances of the same kind as H. P. Blavatsky's theosophical fantasy of an organized fraternity of high initiates in the spiritual and occult sciences, distributed throughout the world, and subtly inspiring and directing every form of positive growth in religion and science. The much less melodramatic truth is probably that within the Roman hierarchy there are a few individuals whose

[1] At least one reason why the religio-sexual orgy (as distinct from a mere rutting rout) is almost wholly impracticable in our culture is that it is virtually impossible to exclude people whose emotional wires are so crossed that they cannot distinguish between the sexy and the dirty. For example, the "dirty-old-man" type who leers and giggles about sex because it fascinates and arouses guilt at the same time.

private opinions about religion would accord approximately with the ideas I have been suggesting all along. However, there would be no sort of organized fellowship between these individuals, and still less would they constitute an official elite in the hierarchy itself. Otherwise, the crudities of the Catechism are acceptable to highly intelligent clergy and laymen because they can be rationalized by extremely sophisticated theological arguments. The trouble is that just the same sort of argumentation can be used to rationalize any proposition whatsoever. One might write—and someone may well have written—a defense of the proposition that insects are the highest manifestation of the divine principle, and that the destiny of man is to evolve into an insect or to be subject to insects, and set it forward in the style of Mgr. Ronald Knox or Fr. M. C. d'Arcy. How else do well-educated people swallow the fantasies of Mormonism or of Swedenborg?

Speculations as to the nature of an esoteric Catholicism, which might claim Meister Eckhart or John Scotus Erigena as its spokesmen, are usually constructed along the lines of Gnosticism, with its heavy emphasis upon the gulf between the spiritual and the material, upon the sole reality of the former, and upon disciplines which lead to release from material existence. This is the rationale whereby, say, the doctrines of the Virgin Birth and the Resurrection of Christ's Body can be understood spiritually rather than physically, and it was from such a standpoint that Origen rationalized the mythology of the Old Testament. It was his frank opinion that, taken literally, much of the Old Testament was simply "puerile."

But Gnosticism is, by and large, far more other-worldly than official Catholicism, and will have no truck whatever with the marriage of spirit and flesh.

Christianity does not, like Hinduism or Buddhism, have an "orthodox" esotericism—a body of traditional doctrine and discipline handed down from master to student, but not disclosed to the general multitude of devotees. There is, perhaps, something approaching this in the art and in the manuals of "spiritual direction." Pious clergy and laity often seek out a particularly holy monk or priests as their "spiritual director," and the wisdom and experience of these directors is set forward in such works as Poulain's *Graces of Interior Prayer,* Scupoli's *Spiritual Combat,* Chapman's *Spritual Letters,* St. Teresa's *Interior Castle,* or that marvelous anthology of Eastern Orthodox spirituality, the *Philokalia.* But these works do not suggest any radical transformation of the sense of dogma. They go along with the usual theological rationalizations and, indeed, often manifest some anxiety lest the aspirant to high states of prayer should lose faith in the literal sense of the Catechism, since the latter is somehow supposed to keep him well grounded—especially in intellectual humility.

No, we must look for the "inner sense" of Christianity in quite other directions. The esoteric aspect of Christianity lies in what must be called, paradoxically, its "unconscious intent," or, perhaps less paradoxically, its "unconscious direction." We can assume an unconscious *intent* if we make the experiment of looking at Christianity within the context of Hinduism, and thus regard the predicament of being a

Christian as a very adventurous role being "played" by the Godhead. Insofar as the Godhead is "lost" in his role, the intent in playing it is forgotten and unconscious. We can assume an unconscious *direction* if we ask, "What will be the actual results of following the Christian way consistently?" I have been trying to show that the Christian way—the challenge of Christ—is a double-bind in that it commands the deliberate enactment of spontaneous behavior, such as love and humility. When this commandment is presented to people who believe that they are separate and independent egos, the rigorous attempt to obey it will result in a paralysis which reveals the ego to be a fiction, and leads on to a new sense of identity. This has, in fact, been the experience of innumerable devout Christians, though the cultural context in which they have lived, together with the Church's official censorship, has forced them to express the new sense of identity in terms consistent with official theology. Thus the Catholic mystic attempting to describe his union with a God who is the transcendent and omnipotent King of kings, literally knowing and controlling all things, has to split hairs most skillfully.

What, then, is the unconscious intent or direction of the Christian attitude to sex? Perhaps this question may well be introduced by a personal reminiscence—of a boy's initiation into the English Church at no lesser shrine than Canterbury—a reminiscence that could be repeated in its essentials by millions of initiates into all brands of Christianity except, perhaps, the most liberal forms of Protestantism.

In very many denominations of the Church the rite of Confirmation corresponds to the puberty and initiation-into-manhood ceremonies of other cultures, since it normally occurs at about the age of fourteen. When it is customary to baptize babies (out of the neurotic fear that unbaptized children will go to a gloomy limbo if they die), Baptism ceases to be the initiation rite, save in potentiality. This potentiality is made actual in the sacrament of Chrism or Confirmation, wherein the individual makes his own conscious and responsible profession of being a Christian. He is then received into active membership of the Church and admitted to the Holy Communion, and this new status is traditionally conferred by a bishop, who anoints the candidate with holy oil and lays hands upon his head.

Confirmation is therefore preceded by some weeks of instruction concerning the doctrines and disciplines of the Church, and in my own experience this was largely taken up with Bible stories and, above all, Church history, for the religion of the British is in some ways a sort of pious archaeology. There is a sense of continuity with a glorious and hallowed past almost unknown in the New World, of companionship with St. Augustine of Canterbury, St. Alban, St. Wilfrid, Edward the Confessor, the Venerable Bede, St. Anselm, St. Thomas à Becket, Edward the Black Prince, Richard Coeur de Lion, and St. Charles the Martyr—a heraldic litany of ringing names whom one comes to regard as one's elder brothers. And the monuments of this past still stand in almost every town and village: cathedrals, abbeys, priories, parish churches and oratories in the enchanted stone of Romanesque (Norman) and Gothic masons. Initiation into the Church is, therefore, a coming into membership with all that these sacred names and monuments represent; and in the background of the English Church there is always the faintly glowing glamour of King Arthur and his Knights, of the mysteries of Chivalry, and of the High Quest of the Holy Grail. In Glastonbury, Wells, Exeter and Tintern it is an almost tangible presence.

Even as a child one would have expected that, beyond this historical pageantry, the core of one's initiatory instructions would have been the revelation of some deep mystery about the nature of God, for, sure enough, every boy to be confirmed was taken apart for a very serious private talk with the school chaplain. Emotionally and dramatically, this was obviously the climax of one's preparation, the moment in which the real secret meaning of the initiation was to be revealed. Naturally, no one kept the secret, and it was well known in advance that the VERY SERIOUS TALK was a grave warning against the evils of masturbation—an act which some of us at that age did not even know how to perform! In addition, then, to some uncertainty as to what we were being warned against, its dire results were defined so vaguely as to give infinite range to the imagination. Thus it was rumored among us that boys who "abused" themselves might shortly contract syphilis, gonorrhea, epilepsy, creeping paralysis, bubonic plague, or the Great Siberian Itch. Boys who thus "played with themselves" were always recognizable by the bags under their eyes, pimples on the chin, and boils on the crotch, and it was expected that their brains would eventually rot and come dripping through their noses.

The timing and the serious atmosphere of this talk left no doubt as to what was really the most important thing in the Christian religion. Since no one was likely to get married for at least ten years, the high and heroic task of Christian life was to take the utmost pains (including cold showers) to avoid paying attention to the little devil between one's legs. One's soul was clean and pure for the Holy Communion, and one was a true and dedicated Knight of the Grail, if one had kept oneself clean—i.e., not masturbated. As simple as that.

Having once been boys themselves, our ecclesiastical and academic superiors were perfectly well aware of the chief and unacknowledged rule of all educational institutions for adolescents. The rule is that one proves and asserts manhood not so much by consistent defiance of authority as by certain acts of ritual defiance to which one is "dared" by one's peers. There is a conspiracy to protect all such acts by silence, and anyone who breaks silence and reports the offense to the authorities is a sneak, tattletale, goody-goody, spoilsport, and, by any name, definitely *not* one of the boys. What, then, is more perfectly suited for a ritual assertion of manhood than masturbation? It is against the rules. It is the male generative act. It is immense fun. And if you half believe the authorities, you can have the most wonderful spasms of guilt and penitence after you have done it.

Since all this was well known to the authorities, why did they go on connecting Confirmation with talks against sex? Of course, in the front of their minds they didn't think about it—and how easy it is to forget one's own childhood! They knew only that this was what their elders and betters had done for them as boys, and that it was their duty to carry on the tradition. But what could have been in the back of their minds?

Let us suppose an entirely different approach. What if the whole matter of sex had been handed over to the school physician, that he had prescribed masturbation once a week as a general health measure, and had explained the entire mechanisms of sex with the aid of plastic models? What if boys and girls were taught to perform intercourse in class, just as they learn dancing? What if such classes were compulsory, and if it were the rule to change partners each time to facilitate adaptibility in sexual adjustment? What if such a program in sexual hygiene were held in a nudist camp, so that all the details of male and female bodies were as familiar as hands and feet? Naturally, this would be the highway to clean, healthy, honest, open, free, guiltless, and perfectly boring sexuality.

It has always been known that "forbidden fruit is sweetest," though the idea that the pleasure of sex is in proportion to its supposed sinfulness is rather too simple to explain the problem. This is indeed part of the picture, and it has often been noted that the repression of sex in Christian cultures has fostered the feeling that nothing in the world is more to be desired than venery. Nowhere else has it struck people to advertise beer, cigarettes, soda water, air travel and undertaking services with the aid of naked or half-naked girls. Nowhere else would the doctrines of Freud have seemed peculiarly significant. As Keyser-

ling once observed, the Christian West has thought
up refinements of lascivious dress without parallel,
and has learned how to protect the private parts of
women with a complexity of corsets, girdles and gar-
ter belts with their marvelous block-and-tackle arrangements for securing silk stockings, frilly panties
and petticoats, bloomers, tights, and chemises—all
of which become thereby sexual fetishes. The more
modest, the more immodest. Repression works on the
principle that the tighter the channel, the stronger
the jet.

All this is obvious enough. Far more important,
however, is the fact that the whole conflict between
prudery and license is a game of "let not your left
hand know what your right hand doeth." In this respect it is an analogue and an aspect of the cosmic
game of hide-and-seek in which the Godhead forgets
itself to seek itself. For when God created the world
what he really said was not, "Let there be light!"
but, "You must draw the line *somewhere*." This was
the dividing of the light from the darkness, the upper
waters from the nether waters, and the heavens from
the earth. It is also the creation of identity, the line
of boundary between this and that, yours and mine,
the ins and the outs, the good guys and the bad guys,
the fair and the foul. At a more complex level, it is
the question of where we draw the line in class dis-
tinctions, in etiquette and manners, in color of skin,
in girth of body, in length of skirts, in area of nudity,
and, above all, in degree of intimacy.

How far will we go with each other? First names?
Holding hands? Kissing? Tongue kissing? Where do
we draw the line as to how far your body may be

familiar with my body? And under what conditions? A hundred dollars a night? Just friends? Going steady? Marriage and babies? Swear to be true to me for always? You must draw the line somewhere. As the seducer plays to lift the lady's skirt higher and higher, so the progressive liberal tries to extend the areas of sexual freedom, to push the line of taboo back and back—and sometimes it seems as if he wanted to get rid of the line altogether. Contrariwise, the reactionary conservative, the square, stuffed-shirt, bluenose, and hidebound traditionalist want, to lower the skirt down to the ground like a nun's habit, and to restrict the area of intimacy to the utmost. Between husband and wife only. For reproduction only. And only in the face-to-face position with the lady beneath, as befits her sex. No divorce allowed. (Seriously, that is the rule of Catholic moral theology.)

Certainly the progressive liberal must not be allowed to have his way entirely. If no lines are drawn there is no creation, no form—only a mass of featureless goo. And, secretly, the liberal does not want there to be no line. No one is more unhappy when the opposition collapses and there are no more squares to be shocked. Equally, the reactionary must not have his way entirely, for he will end up by calling on all of us to be virgins. But, like the liberal, the reactionary does not really want this to happen, because he, too, feels quite at a loss when there is nothing to be shocked about and there are no more sinners to condemn. He has to invent new degrees and minutiae of sin, just as the profligate has to resort to bizarre forms of erotic stimulation.

We do not want a stalemate, a fixed balance between the two sides, for the line of creation is a living line which constantly pulsates and throbs, since all being is plus/minus, up/down, and come/go. Each side must therefore be perpetually winning a little and losing a little, bearing in mind that to win even a little it may be necessary to try to win all. This is approximately how clear forms are produced: the form of a hard surface is a restrained agitation of atoms, just as a fast electric fan seems to merge its blades into a disc. A clear tone is an evenly vibrating tube or string, for there is only a line of sound (represented in notation by the stave line) if there is a steady vibration. The line must be alive. A constant give-and-take between the areas or volumes on either side of it. A steel beam is strong because of the intense rapidity with which it goes in and out of existence.

The world of forms so produced is a *maya*—a trick or illusion in the positive, Hindu sense of these words—because the mutual opposition of sides whereby the line is drawn must seem to be serious. The continuance of life is an energy evoked by the notion that death would be a disaster. I can play chess with myself to the degree that, when I am playing the white side, I can pretend that I am not the same person who plays the black. And so plays the universe.

Thus the squares and prudes firmly believe that they are quite a different kind of people from the profligates and sensualists, having quite other values and motivations. Contrariwise, the profligates see themselves totally opposed to the prudes—as warm,

generous, easy-going and human-hearted, in contrast
to that thin-lipped, cold-blooded, anal-retentive attitude. To the degree, then, that these two become
conscious only of their differences, forgetting altogether that there is some sort of tacit conspiracy between them, the dividing line begins to be dangerously unstable, swinging so violently from pro to
con that the form which it has outlined starts to dis-
integrate. On the other hand, if the prudes and the
profligates begin to be excessively open-minded and
tolerant of each other, the dividing line becomes
flaccid and mushy. In terms of sexual mores, this
would be the puritanism of the nudist colony: nice,
clean, healthy physical relationships. No black lace
underwear nor frilly nighties. Just a sensible diet of
corned beef and cold, boiled potatoes.

A fruitful interplay or contest of opposites always
depends on a *tacit* understanding between the two
sides. That which we all recognize but do not mention, publish, or make official, because to do so would
be spoiling the sport and giving away the show. Under our clothes we are all naked, but there is no need
to insist on it unless it has been altogether forgotten.

In writing this book, I am to some extent letting the
cat out of the bag by publishing things which should
be communicated in secret. But the show will be
saved because it is the simplest thing for officialdom
(i.e., the Church and the Academy) to shrug the
whole thing off as unscholarly, beatnik, disreputable,
and pseudo-Buddhistic. Nevertheless, those who
shrug it off in the classroom will read it in the bath-
room.

The truly esoteric is not, therefore, guarded and

"top secret" information. The esoteric is the tacit. It is what we know in common but do not admit in common, and what we communicate with winks rather than words. At a deeper level, it is also what we know but dare not acknowledge even to ourselves. It must not be admitted that the forces on either side of the line are actually working together; that they need and support each other; that their apparent conflict and independent operation is in fact a single movement seen from opposite points of view. Yet though it must not be explicitly admitted, it must be implicitly understood, just as the differentiation of the spokes at the rim of a wheel is supported by their union in the hub.

It is thus that the Church's intensely negative fascination with sexuality acts as the context and stimulus for a prolific erotic life. It provokes it in the "opposition," in those who rebel deliberately and even more in those who resist temptation to the point where they are at last compelled to give in. It provokes it as much in professing churchmen as in their agnostic and atheistic neighbors, giving Christians a sexual ambivalence which is something far more subtle than mere hypocrisy. Hypocrisy is simply using a mask of righteousness to conceal shameless ill-doing. But sexual ambivalence is an admixture of lust and guilt to the mutual stimulation of both, and it issues in the style of eroticism that we call prurient. For churchly chastity is the obverse of which the inseparable reverse is eroticism with black chiffon panties—salacious, lascivious, lewd and libidinous. The erotic equivalent of a Nightmare Sundae with chocolate fudge, butterscotch, whipped cream, chopped walnuts, marshmallow, and maraschino cherries.

Truly, it is a rather formidable achievement, though as one becomes wiser and more discriminating one looks for the erotic equivalent of a finely grilled trout with chablis.

Here, as in other respects, the Christian situation is an extremity, for just as the Christian soul is the Godhead playing most convincingly that it is *not* God, so in the sexual sphere there is almost complete repression (in prude and profligate alike) of the sense that asceticism and eroticism are mutually fructifying. Hence the extreme shock and horror when it is found out that some particularly holy and respected prelate has been leading a "double life." It seems to reduce him to a pious fraud, but it usually escapes both the tormented cleric and his outraged flock that fraud is something quite different from ambivalence. Fraud may be used to conceal ambivalence when the existence of the latter has been clearly recognized. But our cleric has not been wearing the cloth to conceal his lascivious proclivities; he really believes in all that he preaches, but finds that it is overwhelmingly impossible to practice because the legs of one of his secretaries just refuse to be wiped out of consciousness. Actually, they are quite ordinary legs, but they are (a) possibly attainable, and (b) forbidden by God. Therefore Helen of Troy was not more shapely, and by such magic a passably pretty girl is transformed into a goddess.

If there was any fraud, both the cleric and his flock have defrauded themselves in the sense of falling for the *maya* that sexual desire and ascetic continence are separate and opposed forces. As well expect pruning the trees to dry up the fruit. But they fall for it as we all fall for the trick which our over-reliance on conscious attention plays upon us: that the figure moves independently of the background and the organism of the environment. It is difficult indeed for us to see and feel the two sides moving together as aspects of a single process. We have seen that the false identity of myself as something quite other than the world (environment) may be dispelled if one attempts to act upon it consistently, how, when faced with the challenge of "Thou *shalt* love," the Christian ego is reduced to absurdity. The same kind of absurdity should be apparent in the fact that prurient eroticism increases with the restriction of prudery (and anyone who doubts it should acquaint himself with Victorian pornography).

What happens when we see through the trick? Of course, if you have a penchant for that style of eroticism, you keep quiet and ride the situation for all it's worth. But it will never again be quite so lurid, for the guilt connected with sex vanishes just as soon as you understand the secret connection between lust and chastity. In its unconscious "let-not-your-left-hand-know" form, the Christian sex-game gets out of hand to the point where the price for luscious eroticism is not only a posture of prudery but a vast amount of mere misery and of warped lives. The game is just too far-out. But it should be obvious that if Christianity really means what it says about the union of the Word and the Flesh, the resolution of the problem must be the divinization of sexuality— foreshadowed (one is tempted to say "parodied") in the idea of Holy Matrimony, and in the idea of the Mystical Marriage between Christ and the Church.

Freud, who was essentially a puritan, interpreted religious symbolism as an unconscious manifestation of *libido*, which is, as the choice of the word suggests, *dirty* sex. "Freud," wrote Philip Rieff, "comes to the tacit understanding that sex really is nasty, an ignoble slavery to nature." (22) Theologians have countered with the thought that living for sexual satisfaction as the highest good is a result of repressed religion, that erotic delight is a poor substitute for the ineffable joy of the knowledge of God. Sexual pleasure, they say, is like salt water, quenching thirst only to inflame it the more. In the end it comes to nothing, for man is made so that only the vision of God can satisfy him.

But the proper response would be to turn the tables on Freud: to admit with delight that the church spire is, indeed, a rampant penis; that vescial windows are vaginas; that the font is the womb—*divini fontis utero,* as the Missal says; that the Church's attitude of self-surrender to the Lord is feminine delight in being ravished; that "Thy will, not mine, O Lord" is "and yes I said yes I will Yes!"

Consider what self-immolation and submission to the divine will must be if it is *not* that. Instead of the melting warmth of sexual surrender, there is the shivering child under the lash—the loving lash—for "whom the Lord loveth he chasteneth," saying, "This hurts me more than it's going to hurt you." Surrender of the will is then what happens when the child's spirit is broken. . . . "Stop pouting! Take that look off your face! Don't be a slobbering cry-baby!"

The sacrifices of God are a broken spirit: a broken and contrite heart, O God, thou wilt not despise.

With all the rebellion whipped out of it, the whimpering brat kisses the hand that flogs—but far, far inside rages implacably at this indignity and affront to nature. Wasn't it Madame Acarie, that celebrated holy woman of seventeenth-century Paris, who used to make her daughter kneel down and say the "Our Father" while bending over to be thrashed?

It is easy for us to forget the compassionate concern with which the tortures of the Inquisition were administered. Isn't one justified in going to *any* length to protect someone from those everlasting fires beside which the stake is nothing? After all, the doctors of those times took hell-fire as seriously as they now take cancer. They lay awake at night shuddering at the post-mortem horrors in store for the unrepentant heretic.[2] But of course it cannot be consciously admitted that the writhings of a "witch" at the stake, of a heretic on the rack, or of a child under the lash are a vicarious orgasm. The alternative to open and loving sexuality is secret and brutal sexuality. So long as we cannot see love on the screen, we must see violence.

There is no way of being non-sexual. The Church reeks of sexuality because it is the one thing intentionally and obviously absent, the one thing definitely concealed, and thus the one thing really important.

[2] An idea for some dramatist: a play about the Holy Inquisition in modern dress, with the inquisitors in white coats discussing *heresy* in the jargon of psychiatry. The torture (called "therapy") is the strait-jacket, lobotomy and electro-shock treatment.

Nothing draws attention to the sexuality of a statue more effectively than the improbable growth of a fig leaf from the midst of the pubic hair. The religions of the world either worship sex or repress it; both attitudes proclaim its centrality. To understand the mysteries, always look for what is veiled.

However, the divinization of sex is obviously something very much more than the philosophy that the best thing in life is sexual intercourse, considered as a physiological action. Our difficulty with sexuality is that we regard it as something "merely" physical, the isolated interplay of two organs, culminating in a pleasurable sensation of convulsive detumescence. We have defined, classified and contextualized the sexual relationship in such a way that all our associations with it are confused. We see it as a somewhat grotesque, undignified, more-animal-than-human spasm, which doesn't fit at all well with our image of ourselves as ladies and gentlemen, yet which is nonetheless ungovernably attractive. But all this grotesquerie is "in the mind," in the system of symbolic, artificial and stylized postures which we have been taught to associate with dignity and decency. The constant reiteration of the attitude of "Ugh!" toward sexual matters by parents, teachers, elders and betters, builds this reaction into the nervous system, so that it is taken for natural and normal feeling. By such negative hypnosis even honey can be made to taste of rotten eggs.

Our attitudes toward that most blatant sexual organ, the flower, are just the opposite. Flowers call to mind a world of innocence and light, transparency and joy. They may adorn the altar, be held as exem-

plars of faith ("Consider the lilies"), be symbols of
the Holy Virgin ("I am the Rose of Sharon"), who is
said, moreover, to cultivate a rose garden in Paradise, and even be the image of the transfigured cosmos in that day when it shall reflect the full glory of
its Maker.

> Thus, in the semblance of a snow-white rose,
> There was displayed to me the saintly throng
> That Christ, with his own blood, had made his bride.
> (*Paradiso*, 31.)

Yet the flower is the lust of the plant, opening itself
with the allure of scent and color as if to say, "and
yes I said yes I will Yes!"

If man is supposed to be made in the image of
God, it should follow that human generation has its
archetypal pattern in the divine act of creation. The
Hindus portray this quite openly in images of Shiva
or Krishna with his *shakti* or feminine aspect, em-
bracing him with her legs around his loins. The
shakti is, of course, the *maya*—the world-illusion and
the cosmic play to which the Lord has abandoned
himself, and together the masculine and feminine aspects signify the eternal oscillation of in/out, lost/
found, and yes/no. And this oscillation is also the
vac, the primordial sound or word, AUM, whereby
all things are brought into manifestation, and thus the
equivalent of the Word in Christianity with its two
aspects, Logos, reason, and Sophia, wisdom.

If we can see through the bewitchment of the lust/
guilt, prudery/prurience sex-game, it becomes obvious that the sexual intercourse of human beings
should evoke the same kind of "cosmic wonder" that
we feel for the stars, for mountains, and for all the

timeless marvels of nature, myth and art. Here we step out of the costumes which designate our temporal roles to become again Adam and Eve, Shiva and Parvati, and—why not?—Logos and Sophia, Christ and his Church. The pattern and posture of our bodily union is, after all, essentially the same as the helix form of the spiral nebulae; and, if you really look, human flesh is no less full of light and transparency than petals and shells and alabaster, for "the joints of thy thighs are like jewels, the work of the hands of a cunning workman."

Yet how can sex be thus divinized when our bodies grow old, dry and impotent, when some of us are compelled to be gross, scraggy, or deformed, and when the flesh is ever prone to disease? This is, of course, the most ancient of all complaints about the delights of love. But it goes hand in hand with the identification of the Self with the separate body, so that, when the prime of life has passed, I must say farewell forever to these embraces. The lament about the transiency of fleshly beauty is a half-truth, for the other side of the matter is that love and beauty are always and always returning—every situation of love being the reincarnation of the Primal Pair, somewhat as a particular sonata may be played again and again upon thousands of instruments. We forget that the Self, the identity, is in the pattern, not in the delusive "body" that bears it, and that this is equally true of the very thing that we call the body. For all that we recognize as constant and consistent in any physical body is a repeated pattern of behavior, recurring exactly like the characteristic phenomena of spring, or like the logarithmic spiral in every chambered nautilus. Any permanent material that could bear the imprint of these patterns, so as to be the medium in which they are wrought, has never been discovered. Indeed, if there were some ground or primal substance in and of which all these patterns are formed, it would correspond far more closely to our ideas of God than to our ideas of matter.

All peoples feel a certain sadness with the passing of youth into age—the autumnal mood which the Japanese call *aware*, the mood of the sigh. To the extent, however, that we imagine our very self to be this body alone, once and for all, aging can bring on a furious resentment of physical existence. It is for this reason, then, that the peculiarly isolated situation of the Christian ego gives us an attitude to the physical body that veers between resentful disillusion and frantic attempts to "gather rosebuds while ye may." But as the awareness of oneself goes in and in and in to the Heart behind the heart, it is ever more clear that the core of the Self is held in common between oneself and all others, and that without need for conscious memory to bridge the intervals, our multiform incarnations emerge again and again, like fruits in season, each one, like the sun through a lens, a focus of the One-and-Only.

To know this is, in the terms of the hide-and-seek-game, to have found "home," the "our eternal home" of the Christians, and the liberation or *moksha* of the Hindus. Neither should be taken literally, as, on the one hand, an everlasting church service after death, or, on the other, permanent disappearance from the world of form and manifestation. For the "death" which must be undergone to behold the vision of God is the death of a false identity, and the withdrawal from the world which is required for liberation is withdrawal from the game that this particular person, so-and-so, is my one and only self. For the rest, the vast and splendid electrical fantasy of the universe may go on and on, the same old story repeated with inexhaustible genius for variety—color, music, intricacy of pattern, beauty and terror, love and tragedy, ducks on the dawn water, gulls sailing the gale, horned flames of the fire, and the wonder-jewel of the witnessing eye, all woven out of the endless possibilities of yes-and-no.

VIII

Is It True?

We have been looking at Christianity in the context of the world-view of the Hindus, which is a dramatic, mythological presentation of the cosmos as the hide-and-seek game of the Self. The presupposition is that originally and fundamentally there is but one Self common to us all (and what else is the Common Man?), which is at once *reality*, what there is and all that there is, and one's own being at its deepest level. Just because the Self is the foundation of the universe, and has nothing beyond or outside it, the Self can never be an object of knowledge, nor can there be an accurate conception of its nature expressed in positive and descriptive language. It is much too close for vision. However, the "game" or *lila* of the

Self is, rhythmically and regularly, to forget itself in the creative illusion (*maya*) that it is all these separate beings, things and events which we call the cosmos, in such a way that in and as each being it seems to itself to be that one only. When the game has run its course, the Self awakens to its original identity.

The Christian and theistic world-view, shared to some extent by Jews and Muslims, is that all beings and things are evoked or created by the will of God "out of nothing," which is to say that they are nothing apart from his will that they be. However, they exist on their own in the sense that they are not disguises of the Divine Self, not parts or aspects or manifestations of God, not roles that he is playing. For between the Creator and the creature there is an infinite difference, even though a union between the two may become so intimate that the creature appears to be divinized. But because the creature is fundamentally and absolutely other than the Creator, the creature is always in peril of the final and irremediable disaster of going off on its own way so far as to lose fellowship with its Creator forever. For in the Christian view the angelic and human creatures have the freedom to choose between the love of God and the love of themselves, since love is not love at all unless freely given. (But the Lord says, "You *must* love me!")

We have seen that if the Christian view of the world is true, the Hindu cannot be true. On the other hand, if the Hindu view is true, the Christian can also be true—in the sense that the situation of seeming to be a lonely soul other than God and in peril of damnation could be one of the most extreme and adventurous roles of the Self. Thus the intense seriousness of Christianity represents that moment in the *drama* of existence at which we are persuaded that this is not drama at all but "the real thing." But this is, from at least one point of view, the best moment—the moment when the actor's art deceives the audience, and even, perhaps, himself.

This "Chinese box" inclusion of the Christian myth within the Hindu seems to me more fruitful and suggestive than the alternative of taking the Christian myth to be true, to the exclusion of the Hindu. It is also more complimentary to the Christian position, because it makes it a dramatic triumph instead of a feat of pure dogmatic stubbornness. One realizes that the latter has nicer names: total commitment, the sacrifice of the intellect, unreserved love and obedience to our Lord, etc. But the presupposition that one's own religion is, even without examining others, the best and truest of all is, however named, stupidity.

Having, then, seen what happens to Christianity in this larger context, one will finally ask, "Is it true? Is this the actual situation of man in this universe?"

Throughout this discussion I have spoken of both the Hindu and the Christian cosmologies as "myths," because the form in which they are stated is plainly naïve and anthropomorphic. But Hindu and Christian philosophers alike have far more sophisticated and abstract ways of presenting their doctrines. If we are going to discuss their relative truth, they must bear comparison with yet another sophisticated view of the universe—the vague consensus of scientists. And science, too, has a mythological level, which is the fiercely held position that the physical universe (outside man) is dead and stupid. Man, in this mythology, is the pure fluke of a sensitive intelligence arising in a world that is simply mechanism, and not very efficient mechanism at that. Some would go so far as to say that all the laws and orders of nature are simply tools, like saws and knives and rulers, which the human mind employs to bend the world to its will. We invent the laws of nature as we invent lines of latitude and longitude to determine position upon the chaotic face of land and sea.

In our present intellectual climate, it seems to me simply inept and boorish to claim that a certain philosophical or theological position is "the Truth," and still more so to attempt to prove it. We know enough, today, about logic, about the history of ideas, about the human mind, and about the physical world to know that we know very little for certain. In the domain of immediate spiritual experience we may have had transformations of consciousness and of the sense of identity that are accompanied with a feeling of total certainty. But when such experiences are formulated in language that purports to describe the way things are, we must use great caution. It is one thing to have an authentic vision of the stars, but quite another to deliver an accurate description of their relative positions.

My own feeling is that the most that should be claimed for any metaphysic, theology or cosmology which is trying to say something about the way things are, about how the universe really works, is plausibility. For what one needs in this universe is not certainty but the courage and nerve of the gambler; not fixed convictions but adaptability; not firm ground whereon to stand but skill in swimming. Certainty might well be desirable in a universe where everlasting damnation is a real possibility. But, seriously, is it plausible to conceive our universe as something run on the lines of Egyptian, Persian and Byzantine monarchies, with their thrones and judgments, their dungeons, torture chambers and scaffolds?

To say that the traditional Christian imagery of God as the heavenly King is to be understood as myth rather than fact is not to say that modern science has disproved the existence of such a being. It is only to say that the general climate of twentieth-century knowledge and thought has made it thoroughly implausible and slightly comic. And so long as we are exhorted in church services to address ourselves (for example) "with a pure heart and a humble voice unto the throne of the heavenly grace," the very idea of God will be contaminated with this (now) ridiculous image. It is simply unimaginable that the universe of modern astronomy and physics, biology and chemistry, should be the creation of any such pompous potentate; our world is much too astonishing for any explanation of that kind to be meaningful. As the Bishop of Woolwich has said in his forceful manifesto *Honest to God* (23), the image of a "supranatural" Being "out there," who is in some sense (metaphysical and moral if not spatial) outside his universe, has become a serious liability to Christianity.

To sophisticated theologians it may seem somewhat naïve on the part of a bishop to whip such a dead horse. Centuries ago men like St. Albert and St. Bonaventure, St. Thomas and Nicolas Cusanus (all oddly unquoted by the Bishop) had abandoned any crudely external image of God, insisting that the infinite Being of God is present in its entirety at every point of space and time, and that all such characterizations of God as sitting on a throne, shining with light, feeling wrath or dwelling on high are metaphorical or analogical (cataphatic, to be technical). If we are to go beyond metaphor, they maintained, we can speak of God only in negative terms, for, as St. Thomas said, "the divine essence by its immensity surpasses every form to which our intellect reaches; and thus we cannot apprehend it by knowing what it is." (24) The highest knowledge now accessible to us is to know what it is not. It is therefore said (in apophatic terms) that God is *in*finite, *e*ternal, boundless, formless, bodiless.

Yet the Bishop of Woolwich is right in feeling that such rarefied notions of God are far from having penetrated the minds of most Christians, for he recognizes that the image is far more powerful than the concept, and that, to all intents and purposes, the forms of Christianity and the attitudes of Christians suggest that their God is still the Old Gentleman in the sky. Furthermore, setting aside such quasi-heretics as Erigena and Eckhart, even the most rarefied orthodox ideas of God insist to the end that there is some sort of ultimate gulf between the divine Being and the deepest center of one's own being. Even the Bishop wants to keep this gap open.

The Biblical affirmation that is built into the very structure of our relationship to the ground of our being [i.e., God] is an indestructible element of personal freedom. We are not like rays to the sun or leaves to the tree: we are united to the source, sustainer and goal of our life in a relationship whose only analogy is that of *I* to *Thou*—except that the freedom in which we are held is one of utter dependence. (25)

Is this the ultimate consolation—to know that reality is Someone Else who cares? Is the alternative the nightmare of Chesterton's *Mirror of Madmen*?

I dreamed a dream of heaven, white as frost,
The splendid stillness of a living host;
Vast choirs of upturned faces, line o'er line.
Then my blood froze; for every face was mine.

Spirits with sunset plumage throng and pass,
Glassed darkly in the sea of gold and glass.
But still on every side, in every spot,
I saw a million selves, who saw me not.

I fled to quiet wastes, where on a stone,
Perchance, I found a saint, who sat alone;
I came behind: he turned with slow, sweet grace,
And faced me with my happy, hateful face.

I cowered like one that in a tower doth bide,
Shut in by mirrors upon every side;
Then I saw, islanded in skies alone
And silent, one that sat upon a throne.

His robe was bordered with rich rose and gold,
Green, purple, silver out of sunsets old;
But o'er his face a great cloud edged with fire,
Because it covereth a world's desire.

But as I gazed, a silent worshipper,
Methought the cloud began to faintly stir;
Then I fell flat, and screamed with grovelling head,
'If thou hast any lightning, strike me dead!

'But spare a brow where the clean sunlight fell,
The crown of a new sin that sickens hell.

Let me not look aloft and see mine own
Feature and form upon the Judgment-throne.'

Then my dream snapped: and with a heart that leapt
I saw across the tavern where I slept,
The sight of all my life most full of grace,
A gin-damned drunkard's wan half-witted face. (26)

Indeed, if the Face upon the Throne turns out to be
no more than the mask of one's own personality, and
if the knowledge behind it were to amount to no
more than the contents of one's own conscious ego,
one might perhaps scream, "If thou hast any lightning, strike me dead!"

But I have always felt that the real root of the
Christian concern that God should be *other* (Thou)
lies in a confusion about what is oneself (I). The
more we are accustomed to restrict the self to the
faculty and the contents of conscious attention, the
more it must seem that there are whole areas in me
that are beyond me, because the conscious ego does
not control, let alone understand or produce, all those
psycho-physical processes upon which it depends. It
is thus that they seem other and the workmanship of
another, and, as the psalmist sang, "It will praise
thee; for I am fearfully and wonderfully made." Yet
if the definition of the self can include areas outside
normal consciousness and its control, it would not be
necessary to jump to the conclusion that the fearful
and wonderful processes of my inmost being are the
work of Someone Else.

Centuries before Western psychology invented the
idea of the unconscious aspect of one's "own" mind,
Indian and Chinese philosophers devised experi-

ments whereby consciousness could be expanded or deepened so as to include vast areas of experience entirely ignored (or "screened out") by conscious attention, as we are normally taught to use it. While it is true that Jewish, Islamic and Christian mystics had their own spiritual exercises and their own experiences of expanded consciousness, they never really began to work out a "geography" of the inner man comparable to the very careful and detailed studies of Hindu and Buddhist philosophers. On the contrary, Western theology is quite remarkably taciturn about the nature of man's soul and spirit.

It was from such experiments that the Indians and the Chinese derived their sense of unity and continuity between the depths of man (*atman*) and the depths of the universe (*Brahman*). On the other hand, the Jewish-Christian-Islamic world lacked this experimental approach, and, indeed, violently resisted its emergence.[1] It is thus that the world-view of Western theology is based, not on experimental inquiry, but on scriptural revelation. Even today, some of the most liberal Protestant theologians have a curious, nostalgic way of equating the true with the "Biblical"—as if, during the times when these books were written, men had a surer contact with the divine than at other times, and other places. In turn, the Biblical view of the world seems to be based on an analogy between the order of nature and the order of government according to the style of patrist monar-

---

[1] See Joseph Needham (27) on the alliance of Western mysticism and the experimental methods of natural philosophy as against the purely scriptural authority of orthodox theology.

chies. Obviously, the more plausible of these world-views in the intellectual climate of today will be that which is based on experiment.

However, it must be noted that a considerable number of Christian intellectuals make the Bible or the Church their point of departure by a "leap of faith" that seems to absolve them from any intellectual responsibility for examining the basic premises of their views. I think of an extremely devout and intelligent priest who insisted that it was quite wrong to hold any sort of class or meeting for the free discussion of Christianity, since this would obviously imply that Christianity "might not be true." Or the learned and sophisticated German Lutheran minister who wangled himself into the position that the utterance of God's Word in the Bible had to be taken as a sort of axiom, as a primal judgment which, like the very existence of the brain, necessarily precedes all thinking and judging whatsoever. What is the difference between such positions and the notion that the Authorized or King James version of the Bible, complete with marginal notes, descended with an angel from heaven in 1611? I had the most amazing Fundamentalist uncle who not only took all the marginal notes to be the veritable words of Jehovah, but eventually rejected the Bible because he found a naughty word in it. (*Isaiah* 36:12.)

Such weird feats of intelligence would, however, be rationally comprehensible (by current standards) if the acceptance of some such fundamentalist view of the universe could be taken as the same thing as the acceptance of the rules of a game. To play a game, one must not keep questioning the rules. Manifestly, it is quite possible to get along in the world and lead a meaningful life as a Three-Seed-in-the-Spirit Baptist, but in just the same way as one might be a professional golfer or bridge player. For just as every game requires some rules, life itself requires such rules as the grammar of language, civil laws, conventional weights and measures, and a common calendar. But we do not ask whether the dollar-decimal measure of money is more or less *true* than the measure of pounds, shillings and pence. We ask whether it is more or less *convenient*. There is, of course, the very special game of making the best of the most inconvenient rules: how much can one say in the strict form of the sonnet, or how marvelous a carving can be made with a penknife? Yet the idea of convenience is slippery, since it really means no more than the *conveniens,* the coming-together or agreement about certain ends. Convenience is hardly ever the merely utilitarian, the consensus as to what is more or less conducive to survival. We do not want to survive *merely,* or to survive so as to be tormented forever in hell. We want to survive interestingly, even elegantly.

Therefore, all questions of religion and ethics are really questions as to what are optimal game rules. For this is also the question about the very forms and species of life, as to the respective merits of the dinosaur-game, the bee-game, and the man-game. All these variations of life are games and are, in turn, sub-games in a game that includes the rule that "variety is the spice of life." If this is at first objectionable, try the experiment of looking at ferns, angelfish, giraffes, spiders, radiolaria, butterflies, lemons and tadpoles as different dances—waltz, minuet, charleston, rumba and twist, and then you can see them as plays of the same kind as whist, chess, backgammon, solitaire, crossword puzzles and, even, Russian roulette. "Did you ever see a lady go this way, go that way?" That is why the Buddhists call a truly enlightened man a *tathagata*, which means one who comes, or goes, *thus*. "He went thataway."

> This is the way we go to school,
> Go to school, go to school!

To be a Tathagata is to dance the day instead of working it. The "curse of work" that came with the Fall was the supposition that one *must* live. The constrictions and spasms of dying are felt as a frightful agony and a dreadfully serious occasion to the degree that one has been persuaded (a) that you arise in this world once and once only, and (b) that to live is a moral compulsion and duty as well as an ingrained and ineradicable instinct.

Aunt Bessie dying of cancer: not a simple matter at all—not an allowed and lovingly accepted or socially respected series of convulsions, but a ghastly denial of Aunt Bessie as a complicated clotheshorse, earnest churchwoman and dignified fuddy-duddy, hushed into death in a horrible nursing home where the grave demeanor of doctors and nurses and the sensible, clean ugliness of the rooms, and the thought of the Lord waiting as the kindly but ever-so-honestly just Judge at the end of the line, all add up to a death as grotesquely contrived as the emplattered lips of Ubangi women. Leaves may get cold and brown; cats may run into the woods and curl up in a hole; birds may drop into the grass. But when people die, it's *you*—the amazing accumulation of memories, attitudes, postures, possessions and proprieties—that's now going to fall apart, swell, burst or rot in flat contradiction to the image of a person that has been foisted upon you, with your connivance. You must not rot naturally, like a fallen apple.

The community based on mutual assistance makes for a richer and more elegant game than the community based on mutual competition; indeed, without the undergirding of the former, the latter game will not work because it has self-contradictory rules. The Ptolemaic cosmology, and the theology that goes with it, won't work well as a game for the same kind of reason that a top-heavy building won't stand. For the Ptolemaic cosmology envisions the universe as a star turned inside-out, with its rays coming from a nowhere all around to the center. The *middle* of things is the finite, created world; and—in Dante's version—the center of that world is Hell, and Satan himself is the worm that penetrates the world at the "point to which all weights are drawn from everywhere." The world which is created out of nothing, which comes into Being, as distinct from manifesting Being, looks like this:

1. Coming into Being

Instead of this: *Or this:*

2. Manifestation
   of Being

3. Manifestation
   (figure 2)
   involuted

Intelligent Christians no longer hold to the Ptolemaic cosmology; and, thus, as the Bishop of Woolwich points out, we have become accustomed to transposing all references to God and Heaven as "up" and "above" into some sense of "beyond." It may be that the divine is present in the same space that we inhabit, but upon some immeasurably higher level of vibration. Yet God will remain somehow remote and "out there" unless, as Tillich suggests, there is a complete turnabout in which all references to the high and the beyond are translated into terms of *depth*.

The name of this infinite and inexhaustible depth and ground of all being is *God*. That depth is what the word *God* means. And if that word has not much meaning for you, translate it, and speak of the depths of your life, of the source of your being, of your ultimate concern, of what you take seriously without any reservation. . . . For if you know that God means depth, you know much about him. You cannot then call yourself an atheist or unbeliever. For you cannot think or say: Life has no depth! Life is shallow. Being itself is surface only. If you could say this in complete seriousness, you would be an atheist; but otherwise you are not. He who knows about depth knows about God. (28)

But why is the idea of God as the deep more plausible, more acceptable to a modern way of thinking, than the idea of God as the Most High? We are accustomed, also, nowadays to speaking of ingenious and interesting conceptions as "profound" and "deep" rather than "lofty" and "elevated."

On the one hand, Tillich is associating the deep with the weighty and the grave in thinking of God as "what you take seriously without any reservation." The domain of God is the domain of "ultimate concern," since the dimension of depth is where we address ourselves to what *really matters,* to what is "no laughing matter," and also confront (though that doesn't seem to be the right way of approach to the deep) the *mysterium tremendum*—the interior strangeness of Being that makes us shudder and wonder.

I am afraid Tillich's God is, for all the transposition into depth, still—morally speaking—the old God "out there," the Protestant-Biblical Jehovah who lacks real depth to the extent that he lacks humor. Does anyone really want the End, the Final Ground of all things, to be *completely* serious? No twinkle? No gaiety? Something rigid and overwhelming and ponderously real? Such a profound seriousness might be the anteroom, but not the presence chamber.

On the other hand, the real force of Tillich's insistence on depth is surely that it makes God *central* to the universe. The image of creatures radiating from

God is more elegant and more organic than the image of their crawling around beneath his surveillance. This is why the Indian image of the universe as a manifestation or emanation of the divine is such a simple and plausible game-form, especially because it includes all the noble and wonderful possibilities of tragedy, limitation and differentiation without, however, allowing them to overwhelm the ultimate and basic unity. It permits gut-shaking seriousness up to the very last micro-second—to the bullet in the brain, or to the twist of some demon's red-hot trident in the tenderest vitals of a hypocrite in hell, so that just beyond the point when everything reaches final and perfect evil, the scream turns suddenly into the ringing voice that says, "I am Alpha and Omega, the Beginning and the End!"

The theistic image of creatures coming into being, coming into relation to the world out of nowhere at all is, if you really think it through, a freak of imagination without any parallel in nature. Even though two persons or two things may be said to be "poles apart," the very fact that they are poles implies fundamental and original relationship. Nature is always differentiated unity, not unified differences. The universe is not a huge collection of cosmic flotsam and jetsam that came from somewhere else altogether. Such notions are simply against the brain, and defy the pattern of all known physical processes. Theism regards the world as an immense orphanage in which we are only "sons by adoption and grace," and then only if one is lucky enough to get the grace. Thought and imagery cannot actually express the thing that many theologians are trying to say: that we exist solely by the divine will and are yet something quite other than that will. If you say it cleverly enough, it sounds like a very profound paradox. And there is nothing to show that it is any more than that. It is the perfectly schizophrenic idea of the cosmos— brave, but not ultimately plausible. Also not quite brave enough, for how many Christians will dare, at the last gasp, to omit the insurance premium of "God be merciful to me, a sinner!"

People who think in terms of biological forms, organism-environment relationships, electromagnetic fields, and structures of space will naturally be biased to unitary, interrelational or transactional images of the cosmos. It is quite against the grain of their reason to look for models of the universe in the arts of pottery and carpentry, to imagine the world as a mass of inert material, like clay, which requires an external force and intelligence to mold it into form and to drive it into motion. "Remember, O man, that *thou art dust, and unto dust thou shalt return!*" The Christian *tat tvam asi*. The problem for theology has always been to construct a universe which does not make God responsible for sin, but it solves the Problem of Evil by replacing it with the still more formidable problem of creating the world out of nothing, and of a sinless God who does not take responsibility for the separate centers of responsibility which he himself has created. It attempts to affirm the freedom and the value of each individual person by the desperate expedient of souls everlastingly other than God—as if there could be no real and meaningful music unless the individual notes in a melody were to sound all the time. Christian theology has, in short, been using a model of the universe which makes an enthrallingly dramatic game, but when one tries to make out that this is really and finally the way things are, reason must be tortured to the limit to hold the position. Read any first-rate apologist—Maritain, Gilson, C. S. Lewis, Ferré, Barth, Niebuhr—and see with what labored intricacy they leap through the hoops.

Admittedly, a unitary, relational and emanationist model of the cosmos may be more plausible today than that of a constructed artifact. But what of the God or Godhead at the root of things? Any kind of God—the personal, supracosmic ego of the theists, or the impersonal being-consciousness-bliss (*sat-cit-ananda*) of the Hindus? It is no longer of much force to object to an idea of God because it is either anthropomorphic or "man-made." *All* ideas of the universe are anthropomorphic, because they are representations of the world in terms of the human mind. Furthermore, a universe which grows human beings is as much a human, or humaning, universe as a tree which grows apples is an apple tree. "Do figs grow on thistles or grapes on thorns?" is also asking whether people grow on blind mechanism. There is still much to be said for the old theistic argument that the materialist-mechanistic athetist is declaring his own intelligence to be no more than a special form of unintelligence. Uncomplimentary remarks about the universe return like boomerangs to the parts of the universe that make them.

To construct a God in the human image is objectionable only to the extent that we have a poor image of ourselves, for example, as egos in bags of skin. But as we can begin to visualize man as the behavior of a unified field—immensely complex and comprising the whole universe—there is less and less reason against conceiving God in *that* image. To go deeper and deeper into oneself is also to go farther and farther out into the universe, until, as the physicist well knows, we reach the domain where three-dimensional, sensory images are no longer valid. (These are, of course, *graven* images.) For the three-dimensional world seems to appear in a matrix as different from it in form as tones from the flute, as ideas from brain structure, or as a broadcast concert from the electronic apparatus of the radio. Nothing in the information conveyed in the ordinary run of television programs tells us anything about the mechanisms of television. These are almost deliberately concealed. We do not televise through camera 2 a picture of camera 1 televising the show! For what, in the meantime, would be happening to the picture on camera 1?

Thus the idea of an invisible and intangible Ground underlying and producing everything that we sense directly is a situation of just the same kind as that the structure of one's own retina and optic nerves is not in the contents of vision. It is really no problem for an intelligent human being of the twentieth century to conceive that all his experience of the world, together with the world itself, subsists in some kind of unifying and intelligent continuum. (Think of the vast variety of sound—voice, string, woodwind, drum, brass—reproducible on the diaphragm of a loud-speaker.)

The real theological problem for today is that it is,

first of all, utterly implausible to think of this Ground as having the monarchical and paternal character of the Biblical Lord God. But, secondly, there is the much more serious difficulty of freeing oneself from the insidious plausibility of the mythology of nineteenth-century scientism, from the notion that the universe is gyrating stupidity in which the mind of man is nothing but a chemical fantasy doomed to frustration. It is insufficiently recognized that this is a vision of the world inspired by the revolt against the Lord God of those who had formerly held the role of his slaves. This reductionist, nothing-but-ist view of the universe with its muscular claims to realism and facing-factuality is at root a proletarian and servile resentment against quality, genius, imagination, poetry, fantasy, inventiveness and gaiety.[2] Within twenty or thirty years it will seem as superstitious as flat-earthism.

Actually, the sense of being an intelligent and sensitive accident in a doltish universe is an attitude that could arise only in the ruins of theism. For if one begins by looking at the world, not as the form of God, but as some non-divine object, some mechanism made by God, what happens when God dies? The world is felt as mechanism without mechanic. When God is dead, man, who was always defined as a creature other than God, begins to feel himself as other than reality—a sentimental irregularity in a dog-eat-

[2] "A proletarian and a poor man," writes Josef Pieper, "are not the same. A man may be poor without being a proletarian: a beggar in mediaeval society was certainly not a proletarian. Equally, a proletarian is not necessarily poor: a mechanic, a 'specialist' or a 'technician' in a 'totalitarian work state' is certainly a proletarian. . . . The proletarian is the man who is fettered to the process of work." (29)

dog system that might have been contrived by the Devil, if Devil there were. Men so at odds with their environment must either bulldoze it into obedience or destroy it. The two choices come to the same thing.

But a superior religion goes beyond theology. It turns toward the center; it investigates and feels out the inmost depths of man himself, since it is here that we are in most intimate contact, or rather, in *identity* with existence itself. Dependence on theological ideas and symbols is replaced by direct, non-conceptual *touch* with a level of being which is simultaneously one's own and the being of all others. For at the point where I am most myself I am most beyond myself. At root I am one with all the other branches. Yet this level of being is not something to be grasped and categorized, to be inspected, analyzed or made an object of knowledge—not because it is taboo or sacrosanct, but because it is the point *from* which one radiates, the light not before but within the eyes.

If this is that theological bugbear, pantheism, what of it? One is not equating omniscience with conscious attention or the Godhead with the ego. It is simply an assertion of the perennial intuition of the mystics everywhere in the world that man has not dropped into being from nowhere, but that his feeling of "I" is a dim and distorted sensation of That which eternally IS. In the wake of so many centuries of theological monarchism, plus the recent and persuasive nihilism of certain scientists, it may take some courage to accept so bold an assurance. This is not, however, the mere acceptance of a new belief. It could be that, if that is all one can manage. But I have been trying to suggest all along that this is what one must come to by following the Christian way intently and consistently until one realizes the full absurdity of its (and one's own) basic assumptions about personal identity and responsibility.

Nevertheless, I have already suggested that the way in which we *interpret* mystical experience must be plausible. That is to say, it must fit in with and/or throw light upon the best available knowledge about life and the universe. As we enter the latter half of the twentieth century, there seem to me to be three main trends in scientific thought which are at once three ways of expressing the same idea, and three ways of *describing* the identity of things or events as the mystic *feels* them.

The first is the growing recognition that causally connected or related events are not separate events, but aspects of a single event. To describe a causal relation is a fumbling way of recognizing that cause A and effect B go together in the same way as the head and the tail of a cat. This implies that earlier events may often depend in some way upon later events, somewhat as an electric impulse will not depart from the positive pole until the negative pole is established or connected, or as the meaning of a word in a sentence is determined by words that follow. Compare, "That is the bark of a tree," with, "That is the bark of a dog." The sentence as a whole is the event which determines the function and meaning of the "separate" words. Perhaps the best illustration of this way of understanding causality is that the event *rainbow* does not occur without the simultaneous presence of sun, atmospheric moisture, and an observer—all in a certain angular configuration. If any one of the three is absent, there is no rainbow. This may be difficult to understand in the case of the absence of an observer unless one remembers that every observer sees the rainbow in a different place. Where, then, *is* the rainbow? A little consideration will show that something of the same kind must be true of *all* experiences, not only of flimsy and transparent luminescences, but also of such apparently solid things as mountains.

The second is the tendency to think of the behavior of things and objects as the behavior of *fields*—spatial, gravitational, magnetic or social. The reason is that careful and detailed description of the behavior or movement of a body must *also* involve description of the behavior of its environment or surrounding space. Where, then, does the behavior start? Inside the body, or outside it in the surrounding space? The answer is in both and neither, because it is best to abandon the body *and* the space for a new descriptive unit, the body-space, the organism-environment, the figure-ground. It is important to distinguish this way of looking at things from old-fashioned environmental determinism, which describes the organism as moved *by* the environment rather than moving *with* it.

The third, long familiar to biologists, is what Ludwig von Bertelannfy has called Systems Theory. This is approximately that the structure and behavior of any system is only partially accounted for by analysis and description of the smaller units that allegedly "compose" it. For what any of these units is and does depends upon its place in and its relation to the system as a whole. Thus blood in a test tube is not the same thing as blood flowing in veins. For an organism disposes itself in and as various parts; it is not composed of them as one puts together tubes, wires, dials and condensers to make a radio.

These are, then, three ways of approaching the world as a unitary and relational system which are highly useful in the sciences but strangely unfamiliar to common sense. For the latter derives from political, constructionist and mechanical models of nature which, in turn, strongly influence our sensation of the person as an enclosed unit of life excluded from the world outside. But these unitary, relational, and "fieldish" ways of thinking in the sciences give immense plausibility to non-dualist or pantheist (to be frightfully exact, "pan*en*theist") types of metaphysic, and to theories of the self more-or-less akin to the "multisolipsism" of the Hindu *atman*-is-*Brahman* doctrine.

When, for example, we consider the full implications of the way in which we see the rainbow, and realize that this is *also* the way in which we perceive the clouds, the sun, the earth and the stars, we find ourselves strangely close to the "idealism" of Mahayana Buddhism, Berkeley, and Bradley—but with the great advantage of being able to describe the situation in physical and neurological terms, and no gobbledy-gook about "minds" and "souls" to offend the prejudices of the tough-minded or (should I say?) hard-headed. And to such as these the subjective experiences of the mystics are always suspect, for might they not be *distortions* of consciousness brought about by stress, self-hypnosis, fasting, hyperoxygenation or drugs? There is, then, a more structural and

objective foundation for that leap of faith in which
a man may dare to think that he is not a stranger in
the universe, nor a solitary and tragic flash of awareness in endless and overwhelming darkness. For in
the light of what we now know in physical terms, it
is not unreasonable to wager that deep down at the
center "I myself" is "It"—as in "as *it* was in the beginning, is now and ever shall be, world without
end."

If this is a hope, or a fervent belief, Krishnamurti
is right in saying that it should be challenged and
tested with the question, "Why do you want to believe that? Is it because you are afraid of dying, of
coming to an end? Is this identification with the cosmic Self the last desperate resort of your ego to continue its game?" Indeed, if this Supreme Identity is,
for me, a belief to which I am clinging, I am in total
self-contradiction. Not only is there no sense in clinging to what I am; the very act of clinging also implies
that I do not really know that I *am* it! Such belief is
merely doubt dressed up. The final meaning of negative theology, of knowing God by unknowing, of the
abandonment of idols both sensible and conceptual,
is that ultimate faith is not in or upon anything at all.
It is complete letting go. Not only is it beyond theology; it is also beyond atheism and nihilism. Such
letting go cannot be attained. It cannot be acquired
or developed through perseverance and exercises, except insofar as such efforts prove the impossibility of
acquiring it. Letting go comes only through despera-
tion. When you know that it is beyond you—beyond
your powers of action as beyond your powers of re-
laxation. When you give up every last trick and de-

vice for getting it, including this "giving up" as something that one might *do*, say, at ten o'clock tonight. That you cannot by any means do it—that IS it! *That* is the mighty self-abandonment which gives birth to the stars.

REFERENCES

1. Evelyn Underhill, *Worship*. Harper. New York, 1936. p. 38.
2. From "Five-Finger Exercises" in T. S. Eliot, *The Complete Poems and Plays, 1909–1950*. Harcourt, Brace. New York, 1958. p. 93.
3. Shankara, commentary on *Kena Upanishad*. In René Guénon, *Man and His Becoming*. Luzac. London, 1945. p. 114.
4. See my *Two Hands of God*. Braziller. New York, 1963. pp. 37–41. Plates 6–11.
5. D. T. Suzuki (trans.), *Lankavatara Sutra*. Routledge. London, 1932. p. 223. [Ch. 9, 260.]
6. Heinrich Zimmer, *Myths and Symbols in Indian Art and Civilization*. Pantheon Books. New York, 1946. p. 15.
7. St. Thomas, Opusc. lxviii, *in libr. Boetii de Hebdom*.
8. R. M. French (trans.), *The Way of a Pilgrim & the Pilgrim Continues His Way*. Harper. New York, n.d. [1952+]. p. 160.
9. Martin Luther, *Werke Allgemeine*, Vol. I, p. 105. In A. Nygren, *Agape and Eros*, Part II, Vol. II. London, 1939. p. 476*n*.
10. Dom John Chapman, *Spiritual Letters*. Sheed and Ward. London, 1944. p. 145.
11. An excellent introduction to ecological problems is S. P. R. Charter, *Man on Earth*. The Tides. Sausalito, Cal., 1962.
12. "Before the Anaesthetic or A Real Fright" in John Betjeman, *Selected Poems*. John Murray. London, 1948. p. 95.

13. "Four Quartets: East Coker, III" in T. S. Eliot, *The Complete Poems and Plays.* pp. 126–7 (See above, reference 2.)

14. Dom John Chapman, *Spiritual Letters.* pp. 143–4. (See above, reference 10.)

15. "An Eighteenth-Century Calvinistic Hymn" in John Betjeman, *Continual Dew.* John Murray. London, 1937. p. 29.

16. Iulia de Beausobre, *Creative Suffering.* Dacre Press. London, 1940. p. 35.

17. Anonymous Monk of the Eastern Church, *On the Invocation of the Name of Jesus.* Fellowship of Ss. Alban and Sergius. London, 1953. pp. 17–20.

18. For a full discussion of this theme see A. K. Coomaraswamy, "Symplegades" in M. F. Ashley Montagu (ed.), *Studies Offered in Homage to George Sarton.* New York, 1947.

19. W. O. E. Oesterley and Theodore H. Robinson, *Hebrew Religion.* S. P. C. K. London, 1940. Macmillan. New York, 1940. pp. 156–7.

20. *Kena Upanishad,* 1.7.

21. Quoted in Raynor C. Johnson, *Watcher on the Hills.* Harper. New York, 1959. pp. 84–5.

22. Philip Rieff, *Freud: The Mind of the Moralist.* Viking. New York, 1959. p. 154.

23. J. A. T. Robinson, *Honest to God.* SCM Press. London, 1963.

24. St. Thomas, *Summa Contra Gentiles,* I. xiv.

25. Robinson, *Honest to God.* (See above, reference 23.) pp. 130–1.

26. "The Mirror of Madmen" in G. K. Chesterton, *Collected Poems.* Dodd, Mead & Co. New York, 1944. pp. 327–8.

27. Joseph Needham, *Science and Civilization in China,* Vol. II. Cambridge Univ. Pr., 1956. pp. 89–98. See also Walter Pagel, "Religious Motives in the Medical Biology of the Seventeenth Century," *Bulletin of the (Johns Hopkins) Institute of the History of Medicine,* 1935. pp. 3, 97.

References

28. Paul Tillich, *The Shaking of the Foundations*. Pelican. London, 1962. pp. 63–4.
29. Josef Pieper, *Leisure: the Basis of Culture*. Pantheon, New York, 1952. Revised edition, 1963. p. 37.

INDEX

Index

ABOUT THE AUTHOR

Alan Watts, who held both a master's degree in theology and a doctorate of divinity, has earned the reputation of being one of the most original and "unrutted" philosophers of the century. He is best known as an interpreter of Zen Buddhism in particular, and of Indian and Chinese philosophy in general. He was the author of more than twenty books on the philosophy and psychology of religion, including (in Vintage Books) *Behold the Spirit*; *The Book*; *Does It Matter?*; *The Joyous Cosmology*; *Nature, Man and Woman*; *The Supreme Identity*; *The Way of Zen*; *The Wisdom of Insecurity*; *This Is It*; and *Cloud Hidden, Whereabouts Unknown*. He died in 1973.

VINTAGE BELLES—LETTRES

VINTAGE WORKS OF SCIENCE
AND PSYCHOLOGY